MODERN
AUSTRALIAN FOOD

First published in 2012.
This edition first published in 2014.
Bauer Media Books are published by Bauer Media Limited.

MEDIA GROUP

BAUER MEDIA BOOKS
Publisher Sally Wright
Editorial & food director Pamela Clark
Director of sales, marketing & rights Brian Cearnes
Creative director Hieu Chi Nguyen
Art director & designer Hannah Blackmore
Senior editor Stephanie Kistner
Food editor Lucy Nunes
Food writers Madeleine Jelfs, Abby Pfahl
Marketing manager Bridget Cody
Senior business analyst Rebecca Varela
Business analyst Ashley Metcalfe
Operations manager David Scotto
Production controller Corinne Whitsun-Jones

Published by Bauer Media Books, a division of Bauer Media Ltd,
54 Park St, Sydney; GPO Box 4088, Sydney, NSW 2001.
phone +61 2 9282 8618; fax +61 2 9126 3702
www.awwcookbooks.com.au

Food photographer William Meppem
Food stylist Vivien Walsh
Photochef Adam Cremona
Location photographers Hannah Blackmore, William Meppem

The publisher would like to thank the following for props used
in photography: Murobond Coatings www.murobond.com.au

Printed by 1010 Printing Asia Limited, China.

Australia Distributed by Network Services,
phone 1300 131 169; fax 1300 360 165;
networkcontactus@networkservicescompany.com.au
New Zealand Distributed by Bookreps NZ Ltd,
phone +64 9 419 2635; fax +64 9 419 2634;
hub@spg.co.nz
South Africa Distributed by PSD Promotions,
phone +27 11 392 6065/6/7; fax +27 11 392 6079/80;
www.psdpromotions.com

A catalogue record for this book is available from the
National Library of Australia.

ISBN: 978-1-74245-499-3 (pbk.)

© Bauer Media Limited 2012
ABN 18 053 273 546
This publication is copyright. No part of it may be reproduced or transmitted
in any form without the written permission of the publishers.

To order books
phone 136 116 (within Australia) or
order online at www.awwcookbooks.com.au

Send recipe enquiries to:
recipeenquiries@bauer-media.com.au

THE AUSTRALIAN
Women's Weekly

MODERN
AUSTRALIAN FOOD

Delicious classic & contemporary food from the city, country & coast

BAUER
MEDIA GROUP

CONTENTS

THE AUSTRALIAN TABLE

Australian food is a celebration of the way we live: the generous abundance of country-style cooking, the simplicity of freshly-caught seafood and the vibrant café culture. It is our marriage of food and lifestyle that makes Australian cuisine truly unique.

What we eat has been heavily influenced by our multicultural society. South-East Asian, Japanese, Korean, Indian, Middle Eastern, South American, European and Mediterranean foods all have a place at the Australian table. Over time we have adopted the best ingredients, techniques and flavours from these foreign cultures. Ironically it is this rich diversity for which Australian food is known and loved.

Australians expect high-quality, fresh ingredients. The 'eating local' and organic food movements are gathering momentum. There is a growing trend for shopping at local growers' markets where seasonal, locally-grown fruit and vegetables and organic meats are readily available. Eating seasonally means tastier, more nutritious produce, which is also cheaper as it is at its most abundant. A wealth of artisan cheeses, preserves and smallgoods are also available in Australia reflecting our delight in discovering, sampling and cooking truly fabulous food.

Australian cuisine is not only a story of what we eat, but where and how we enjoy food.

CITY

The urban-living Australian is spoilt for choice;
cafés spill out on to bustling footpaths,
internationally-renowned restaurants sit alongside
growers' markets and trendy food-focused bars.
Expect excellence at even the most humble eateries.

BREAKFAST These deli-inspired breakfasts are smart, sophisticated and quick. Easy to prepare, they make a great morning pick-me-up, especially when served with a strong cup of coffee.

eggs benedict

8 eggs

4 english muffins (260g)

200g (6½ ounces) shaved leg ham

¼ cup finely chopped fresh chives

HOLLANDAISE SAUCE

1½ tablespoons white wine vinegar

1 tablespoon lemon juice

½ teaspoon black peppercorns

2 egg yolks

125g (4 ounces) unsalted butter, melted

1 Make hollandaise sauce.
2 To poach eggs, half-fill a large shallow frying pan with water; bring to the boil. Break one egg into a cup, then slide into pan; repeat with three more eggs. When all eggs are in pan, allow water to return to the boil. Cover pan, turn off heat; stand about 4 minutes or until a light film of egg white sets over yolks. Remove eggs, one at a time, with a slotted spoon and drain on absorbent paper; cover to keep warm.
3 Meanwhile, split muffins in half and toast.
4 Serve muffins topped with ham, poached eggs, sauce and chives.

hollandaise sauce Bring vinegar, juice and peppercorns to the boil in small saucepan. Reduce heat; simmer, uncovered, until liquid is reduced by half. Strain through a fine sieve into small heatproof bowl; cool 10 minutes. Whisk egg yolks into vinegar mixture. Set bowl over small saucepan of simmering water; do not allow water to touch base of bowl. Whisk mixture over heat until thickened. Remove bowl from heat; gradually whisk in melted butter in a thin steady stream, whisking constantly until sauce is thick and creamy.

prep + cook time 50 minutes **serves** 4
nutritional count per serving 40.6g total fat (21.2g saturated fat); 2450kJ (586 cal); 24.2g carbohydrate; 30.8g protein; 2g fibre

french toast

4 eggs

½ cup (125ml) pouring cream

¼ cup (60ml) milk

1 teaspoon ground cinnamon

¼ cup (55g) caster (superfine) sugar

100g (3 ounces) butter, melted

8 thick slices white bread (360g)

2 tablespoons icing (confectioners') sugar

⅓ cup (80ml) maple syrup

1 Whisk eggs in medium bowl, then whisk in cream, milk, cinnamon and sugar.

2 Heat a quarter of the butter in medium frying pan. Dip two bread slices into egg mixture, one at a time; cook bread until browned both sides. Remove french toast from pan; cover to keep warm.

3 Repeat step 2 to make a total of 8 french toasts.

4 Serve toasts dusted with sifted icing sugar and drizzled with maple syrup.

prep + cook time 20 minutes **serves** 4
nutritional count per serving 42.2g total fat (24.8g saturated fat); 3194kJ (764 cal); 79.4g carbohydrate; 15.5g protein; 2.6g fibre
tip You could also use slices of brioche or panettone instead of white bread.
serving suggestion Serve with fresh blueberries.

pear & almond friands

6 egg whites

185g (6 ounces) butter, melted

1 cup (120g) ground almonds

1½ cups (240g) icing (confectioners') sugar

¾ cup (110g) plain (all-purpose) flour

1 small pear (180g), peeled, cored, chopped finely

¼ cup (20g) flaked almonds

1 Preheat oven to 200°C/400°F. Grease 12-hole (⅓-cup/80ml) muffin pan.

2 Whisk egg whites in medium bowl until frothy. Add butter, ground almonds, sifted icing sugar and flour, then pear; stir until combined.

3 Spoon ¼-cups of mixture into pan holes; sprinkle with flaked almonds.

4 Bake friands about 20 minutes. Stand in pan 5 minutes; turn, top-side up, onto wire rack to cool. Dust with icing (confectioners') sugar, if you like.

prep + cook time 35 minutes **makes** 12
nutritional count per friand 19.2g total fat (8.8g saturated fat); 1300kJ (311 cal); 28.8g carbohydrate; 5.3g protein; 1.6g fibre

Melbourne laneway, Victoria

chorizo & manchego rolls

3 cured chorizo sausages (510g), sliced thickly

1 cup (280g) whole-egg mayonnaise

½ teaspoon smoked paprika

8 large bread rolls (600g)

5 hard-boiled eggs, sliced thinly

80g (2½ ounces) baby spinach leaves

150g (4½ ounces) manchego cheese, shaved

1 Cook chorizo in heated oiled large frying pan, in batches, until browned. Drain on absorbent paper.
2 Combine mayonnaise and paprika in small bowl.
3 Split rolls in half; spread mayonnaise mixture over half the roll halves. Top with chorizo, egg, spinach, cheese and remaining roll halves.

prep + cook time 20 minutes **makes** 8
nutritional count per roll 39.9g total fat
(12.6g saturated fat); 3018kJ (722 cal);
60.2g carbohydrate; 28.9g protein; 4.1g fibre
tips Manchego cheese is a sharp, firm Spanish cheese; it can be found in most specialty food stores and delicatessens. You can use parmesan cheese instead, if manchego is not available. Use a vegetable peeler to shave the cheese.

{photograph page 17}

corn fritters with smoked salmon

¼ cup (35g) plain (all-purpose) flour

1 tablespoon rice flour

½ teaspoon baking powder

½ teaspoon mild or smoked paprika

¼ teaspoon salt

1 egg, beaten lightly

¼ cup (60ml) milk

1½ cups (240g) fresh corn kernels

2 green onions (scallions), sliced finely

2 tablespoons finely chopped fresh coriander (cilantro)

cooking-oil spray

1 medium avocado (250g), sliced thinly

100g (3 ounces) thinly sliced smoked salmon

1 Sift flours, baking powder, paprika and salt into medium bowl; gradually whisk in combined egg and milk until mixture is smooth. Stir in corn, onion and coriander; season.
2 Spray heated large frying pan with cooking oil. In batches, drop 1 tablespoon of batter for each fritter into pan; cook fritters until browned lightly both sides.
3 Serve fritters topped with avocado and smoked salmon. Serve with a squeeze of lemon juice, if you like.

prep + cook time 20 minutes **serves** 4
nutritional count per serving 15.3g total fat
(3.6g saturated fat); 1154kJ (276 cal);
20.1g carbohydrate; 12.7g protein; 4.1g fibre
tip You will need to cut the kernels from two small cobs of corn for this recipe.

corn fritters with smoked salmon

banana bread

1 cup mashed banana

1 cup (220g) firmly packed dark brown sugar

2 eggs, beaten lightly

40g (1½ ounces) butter, melted

½ cup (125ml) buttermilk

¼ cup (90g) treacle

1½ cups (225g) plain (all-purpose) flour

1 cup (150g) self-raising flour

2 teaspoons mixed spice

1 teaspoon bicarbonate of soda (baking soda)

1 Preheat oven to 180°C/350°F. Grease 14cm x 21cm (5½-inch x 8½-inch) loaf pan; line base and long sides with baking paper, extending paper 5cm (2 inches) over sides.

2 Combine banana, sugar, eggs, butter, buttermilk and treacle in large bowl; stir in sifted dry ingredients. Do not overmix; the batter should be lumpy. Spoon mixture into pan.

3 Bake banana bread about 1 hour. Stand in pan 10 minutes; turn, top-side up, onto wire rack to cool.

prep + cook time 1 hour 20 minutes **serves** 12
nutritional count per serving 4.1g total fat (2.2g saturated fat); 1064kJ (254 cal); 49.6g carbohydrate; 5.3g protein; 1.8g fibre
tip You need two large overripe bananas (460g) to get the amount of mashed banana required for this recipe.
serving suggestion Serve toasted with butter.

SMALL FOOD The international influence on Australian cooking is arguably at its most apparent in the bite-sized, share-plate, entrée-style food found on many inner-city menus. Choose wontons, empanadas or kingfish carpaccio – they all make perfect post-work, pre-dinner accompaniments to a glass of wine.

pork & garlic chive wrapped prawns

250g (8 ounces) minced (ground) pork

2 tablespoons finely chopped fresh garlic chives

1 fresh small red thai (serrano) chilli, chopped finely

2cm (¾-inch) piece fresh ginger (10g), grated

12 uncooked large king prawns (shrimp) (840g)

12 x 12cm (4¾-inch) square spring roll wrappers

2 tablespoons cornflour (cornstarch)

¼ cup (60ml) water

peanut oil, for deep-frying

1 Combine pork, chives, chilli and ginger in medium bowl; season.
2 Shell and devein prawns, leaving tails intact. Cut along back of each prawn, without cutting all the way through; flatten prawns slightly.
3 Place spring roll wrapper on board; fold one corner up to meet centre. Place one flattened prawn onto wrapper; top prawn with 1 level tablespoon pork mixture. Brush around edges with blended cornflour and the water. Fold wrapper around filling, leaving tail exposed; press edges together to seal. Repeat with remaining wrappers, prawns and pork mixture.
4 Heat oil in wok; deep-fry prawns, in batches, until cooked. Drain on absorbent paper.

prep + cook time 40 minutes **serves** 4
nutritional count per serving 15.7g total fat (3.7g saturated fat); 1359kJ (325 cal); 10.6g carbohydrate; 35.1g protein; 0.4g fibre
serving suggestion Serve with soy sauce or sweet chilli.

kingfish carpaccio

kingfish carpaccio

400g (12½-ounce) piece sashimi kingfish

¼ cup (60ml) lemon juice

1 small red onion (100g), sliced thinly

2 tablespoons extra virgin olive oil

1 cup loosely packed fresh flat-leaf parsley leaves

2 tablespoons drained baby capers, rinsed

1 Tightly wrap kingfish in plastic wrap; freeze 1 hour or until firm.
2 Unwrap fish; slice as thinly as possible. Arrange slices on platter; drizzle fish with juice. Cover; refrigerate 1 hour.
3 Combine onion, oil, parsley and capers in medium bowl.
4 Drain juice from fish; serve with onion mixture.

prep time 30 minutes (+ freezing & refrigeration)
serves 8
nutritional count per serving 5.7g total fat (1g saturated fat); 410kJ (98 cal); 0.9g carbohydrate; 10.5g protein; 0.5g fibre
tips Use whatever firm white sashimi-type fish you like. We found we could slice the partly frozen fish finely using a mandoline or V-slicer.

vietnamese prawn rolls

60g (2 ounces) rice vermicelli noodles

500g (1 pound) cooked medium king prawns (shrimp)

¼ small wombok (napa cabbage) (175g), shredded finely

½ cup loosely packed fresh mint leaves, torn

2 teaspoons light brown sugar

2 tablespoons lime juice

12 x 21cm (8½-inch) rice paper rounds

HOISIN DIPPING SAUCE

½ cup (125ml) hoisin sauce

2 tablespoons rice vinegar

1 Place noodles in medium heatproof bowl, cover with boiling water; stand about 10 minutes or until just tender, drain.
2 Meanwhile, shell and devein prawns; chop prawn meat finely.
3 Using kitchen scissors, cut noodles into random lengths; add to same cleaned bowl with wombok, mint, sugar and juice.
4 Make hoisin dipping sauce.
5 Dip 1 rice paper round into bowl of warm water until soft; place on board covered with tea towel. Top with a little of the prawn meat and noodle filling. Fold and roll to enclose filling. Repeat with remaining rounds, prawn meat and noodle filling.
6 Serve with hoisin dipping sauce.
hoisin dipping sauce Combine ingredients in bowl.

prep + cook time 20 minutes **makes** 12
nutritional count per roll 0.9g total fat (0.1g saturated fat); 326kJ (78 cal); 10.8g carbohydrate; 5.5g protein; 1.7g fibre

{photograph page 26}

vietnamese prawn rolls {recipe page 25}

sang choy bow

2 teaspoons sesame oil

1 small brown onion (80g), chopped finely

2 cloves garlic, crushed

2cm (¾-inch) piece fresh ginger (10g), grated

500g (1 pound) lean minced (ground) pork

2 tablespoons water

100g (3 ounces) shiitake mushrooms, chopped finely

2 tablespoons light soy sauce

2 tablespoons oyster sauce

1 tablespoon lime juice

2 cups (160g) bean sprouts

4 green onions (scallions), sliced thinly

¼ cup coarsely chopped fresh coriander (cilantro)

12 large butter (boston) lettuce leaves

1 Heat oil in wok; stir-fry brown onion, garlic and ginger until onion softens. Add pork; stir-fry until changed in colour.
2 Add the water, mushrooms, sauces and juice; stir-fry until mushrooms are tender. Remove from heat. Add sprouts, green onion and coriander; toss to combine.
3 Spoon pork mixture into lettuce leaves to serve.

prep + cook time 30 minutes **serves** 4
nutritional count per serving 11.5g total fat (3.6g saturated fat); 1112kJ (266 cal); 8.9g carbohydrate; 29.3g protein; 4.1g fibre

pork & prawn wontons

375g (12 ounces) uncooked medium prawns (shrimp)

280g (9 ounces) minced (ground) pork

1.5cm (½-inch) piece fresh ginger (7.5g), grated

1 clove garlic, quartered

1 fresh small red thai (serrano) chilli, chopped coarsely

2 green onions (scallions), chopped coarsely

¼ cup (60ml) chinese cooking wine (shao hsing)

1½ tablespoons light soy sauce

1 teaspoon white (granulated) sugar

1 egg white

40 wonton wrappers

1 Shell and devein prawns, coarsely chop.
2 Process prawn meat, pork, ginger, garlic, chilli and onion until finely minced. Add wine, soy, sugar and egg white; process until combined.
3 Place wonton wrappers on bench; place rounded teaspoons of pork mixture in centre of each wrapper. Brush a little water around edges of each wrapper; bring edges together to seal.
4 Drop wontons, in batches, into a large saucepan of boiling water; boil about 5 minutes or until filling is cooked through. Remove wontons from water with slotted spoon.

prep + cook time 40 minutes **makes** 40
nutritional count per wonton 0.5g total fat
(0.2g saturated fat); 96kJ (23 cal);
1.3g carbohydrate; 2.7g protein; 0g fibre
tip You can freeze uncooked wontons in an airtight container for up to 1 month. No need to thaw them before cooking but they will take a little longer.
serving suggestion Serve with soy sauce.

Chinatown, Sydney, New South Wales

peking duck {recipe page 34}

peking duck

2kg (4-pound) whole duck

⅓ cup (80ml) water

1 tablespoon treacle

1 teaspoon rice vinegar

1 tablespoon dry sherry

1 teaspoon five-spice powder

4cm (1½-inch) piece fresh ginger (20g),
sliced thickly

2 star anise

1 lebanese cucumber (130g)

5 green onions (scallions)

20 peking duck pancakes (200g)

PEANUT & HOISIN SAUCE

2 tablespoons hoisin sauce

1 tablespoon peanut butter

1 tablespoon peanut oil

1 tablespoon sake

1 Wash duck under cold water; pat dry inside and out with absorbent paper. Tie string around neck of duck. Lower duck into large saucepan of boiling water for 30 seconds; remove from pan. Drain well; pat dry with absorbent paper.

2 Preheat oven to 240°C/475°F.

3 Tuck wings under duck. Place duck, breast-side up, on wire rack in large baking dish; brush entire duck with combined water, treacle, vinegar, sherry and five-spice. Place ginger and star anise inside cavity of duck. Roast, uncovered, 10 minutes; turn duck breast-side down. Brush with marinade; roast, uncovered, 10 minutes. Turn duck breast-side up; brush with marinade.

4 Reduce oven to 180°C/350°F; roast, uncovered, brushing occasionally with remaining marinade, about 30 minutes or until duck is cooked as desired.

5 Increase oven to 240°C/475°F; roast duck, uncovered, further 10 minutes or until skin is crisp and browned.

6 Meanwhile, make peanut & hoisin sauce.

7 Place duck on chopping board; remove skin. Slice skin and duck meat thickly.

8 Using teaspoon, remove seeds from cucumber. Cut cucumber and onions into 5cm (2-inch) strips. Cut onion into 5cm (2-inch) length.

9 Serve duck meat and crisp skin with pancakes, cucumber, onion and sauce.

peanut & hoisin sauce Combine ingredients in small bowl.

prep + cook time 1 hour 30 minutes **serves** 4
nutritional count per serving 26.8g total fat
(7.5g saturated fat); 2374kJ (568 cal);
21.8g carbohydrate; 56.6g protein; 3g fibre
tips Packets of peking duck pancakes are available from Asian food shops. Heat pancakes according to packet instructions, or by folding each into quarters and placing in bamboo steamer over simmering water until pliable.

gyozas

325g (10¾ ounces) cabbage, chopped finely

300g (10 ounces) minced (ground) pork

4 green onions (scallions), chopped finely

1 egg, beaten lightly

2 tablespoons japanese soy sauce

1 tablespoon sake

2 teaspoons sesame oil

1 teaspoon caster (superfine) sugar

¼ teaspoon ground white pepper

50 gyoza wrappers

1 tablespoon vegetable oil

1 Combine cabbage, pork, onion, egg, sauce, sake, sesame oil, sugar and pepper in medium bowl. Cover; refrigerate 1 hour.

2 Place one heaped teaspoon of pork mixture in centre of wrapper; wet edge around one half of wrapper. Pleat to seal. Repeat with remaining pork mixture and wrappers.

3 Cover base of large frying pan with water; bring to the boil then add gyozas, in batches. Reduce heat; simmer, covered, 3 minutes.

4 Heat vegetable oil in same cleaned pan; cook gyozas, one side only, uncovered, in batches, until browned and slightly crisp. Drain on absorbent paper.

prep + cook time 30 minutes (+ refrigeration)
makes 50
nutritional count per gyoza 1.2g total fat (0.3g saturated fat); 142kJ (34 cal); 3.4g carbohydrate; 2.1g protein; 0.4g fibre
serving suggestion Serve with combined soy sauce and chilli oil, or with rice vinegar.

Melbourne, Victoria

lemon & ricotta-filled zucchini flowers

250g (8 ounces) ricotta cheese

2 tablespoons finely grated parmesan cheese

1 teaspoon finely grated lemon rind

1 tablespoon lemon juice

1 tablespoon finely chopped fresh mint

2 tablespoons roasted pine nuts

12 zucchini flowers with stem attached (240g)

1 Combine cheeses, rind, juice, mint and nuts in small bowl.

2 Discard stamens from inside zucchini flowers; fill flowers with cheese mixture, twist petal tops to enclose filling.

3 Place zucchini flowers, in single layer, in large bamboo steamer, over large saucepan of boiling water. Steam, covered, about 20 minutes or until zucchini are tender.

prep + cook time 45 minutes **serves** 4
nutritional count per serving 13.4g total fat (5.5g saturated fat); 711kJ (170 cal); 2.2g carbohydrate; 9.6g protein; 1.4g fibre
tip Zucchini flowers wilt and spoil quickly. Look for flowers with green, moist stems that haven't dried out at all and bright orange flowers that haven't started to wilt. If you need to store them, keep them chilled and loosely wrapped in a plastic bag. Be sure to put them where they won't be crushed by other produce.

gözleme

4 cups (600g) plain (all-purpose) flour

1 teaspoon coarse cooking (kosher) salt

1⅔ cups (410ml) warm water

2 tablespoons vegetable oil

LAMB FILLING

1 tablespoon vegetable oil

2 teaspoons ground cumin

½ teaspoon hot paprika

3 cloves garlic, crushed

500g (1 pound) minced (ground) lamb

400g (12½ ounces) canned diced tomatoes

½ cup coarsely chopped fresh flat-leaf parsley

SPINACH & CHEESE FILLING

300g (9½ ounces) spinach, trimmed, shredded finely

250g (8 ounces) fetta cheese, crumbled

1 cup (100g) coarsely grated mozzarella cheese

1 small brown onion (80g), chopped finely

½ cup coarsely chopped fresh mint

½ teaspoon ground allspice

1 Combine flour and salt in large bowl. Gradually stir in the water; mix to a soft dough. Knead dough on floured surface about 5 minutes or until smooth and elastic. Return to bowl; cover.
2 Make lamb filling.
3 Make spinach & cheese filling.
4 Divide dough into six pieces; roll each piece into 30cm (12-inch) square. Divide spinach & cheese filling among dough squares, spreading filling across centre of squares; top each with equal amounts of lamb filling. Fold top and bottom edges of dough over filling; tuck in ends to enclose.
5 Cook gözleme, both sides, over low heat on oiled grill plate, brushing with oil, until browned lightly and heated through. Serve with a squeeze of lemon juice.

lamb filling Heat oil in large frying pan; cook spices and garlic until fragrant. Add lamb; cook, stirring, until browned. Add undrained tomatoes; simmer about 15 minutes or until liquid is almost evaporated. Stir in parsley.

spinach & cheese filling Combine ingredients in medium bowl.

prep + cook time 1 hour serves 6
nutritional count per serving 29.9g total fat (12.7g saturated fat); 3168kJ (758 cal); 75.8g carbohydrate; 41.8g protein; 7.1g fibre
tips You can't get much more traditionally Turkish than this combination of lamb, spinach and fetta. You can also try cooking these in a sandwich press – it works beautifully.

pork rillettes with witlof & cornichons {recipe page 46}

pork rillettes with witlof & cornichons

1kg (2 pounds) boned pork belly, rind removed, cut into chunks

3 bay leaves

2 cloves garlic, chopped coarsely

¼ cup (60ml) dry white wine

¼ cup (60ml) water

2 teaspoons salt

1 teaspoon ground black pepper

1 small red onion (100g), chopped finely

1 tablespoon finely chopped fresh flat-leaf parsley

6 witlof (belgian endive) (750g), trimmed, leaves separated

⅔ cup (120g) drained cornichons and pickled onions

1 Preheat oven to 150°C/300°F.
2 Combine pork, bay leaves, garlic, wine, the water, salt and pepper in large shallow baking dish.
3 Roast pork mixture, covered, about 2½ hours or until pork is very tender.
4 Discard bay leaves from pork; using two forks, shred pork finely in dish with pan juices. Stir in onion and parsley.
5 Serve pork mixture with witlof and cornichons.

prep + cook time 3 hours **serves** 8
nutritional count per serving 28.1g total fat (9.5g saturated fat); 1551kJ (371 cal); 3.1g carbohydrate; 24.5g protein; 2.8g fibre
tips We used a bottled mixture of cornichons and baby pickled onions. Rillettes are a classic dish served for an aperitif with slices of baguette, cornichons and a glass of red wine. Duck or goose rillettes are also very popular in France.

{photograph page 45}

chorizo & chickpeas in white wine

1 tablespoon olive oil

1 small brown onion (80g), sliced finely

2 cloves garlic, crushed

2 cured chorizo sausages (340g), chopped coarsely

1 medium red capsicum (bell pepper) (200g), sliced finely

400g (12½ ounces) canned chickpeas (garbanzo beans), rinsed, drained

½ teaspoon smoked paprika

¼ cup (60ml) dry white wine

⅓ cup (80ml) chicken stock

1 Heat oil in large frying pan; cook onion, garlic and chorizo, stirring, until chorizo is browned lightly.
2 Add capsicum, chickpeas and paprika; cook, stirring, until capsicum is tender. Add wine and stock; cook, stirring, until liquid is reduced by half. Season to taste.

prep + cook time 25 minutes **serves** 6
nutritional count per serving 21.1g total fat (6.8g saturated fat); 1241kJ (297 cal); 9.6g carbohydrate; 14.6g protein; 3g fibre
tip This recipe is suitable to freeze.

chorizo & chickpeas in white wine

cod & olive fritters

625g (1¼ pounds) salted cod fillet, skin on

3 medium potatoes (600g), halved

1 tablespoon olive oil

1 medium brown onion (150g), chopped finely

2 cloves garlic, crushed

¼ cup finely chopped fresh flat-leaf parsley

½ cup (60g) seeded green olives, chopped finely

1 egg

vegetable oil, for deep-frying

1 Rinse fish under cold water to remove excess salt. Place fish in large bowl, cover with cold water; refrigerate, covered, overnight, changing the water three or four times. Drain fish; discard water.
2 Place fish in large saucepan, cover with cold water; bring to the boil uncovered. Reduce heat, simmer, covered, 5 minutes. Drain fish, discard water; remove skin and bones then flake fish.
3 Boil, steam or microwave potato until tender; drain. Roughly mash potato in large bowl.
4 Meanwhile, heat olive oil in large frying pan; cook onion and garlic, stirring, until onion softens.
5 Combine fish, onion mixture, parsley, olives and egg with potato; mix well.
6 Roll level tablespoons of fish mixture into balls, place on baking-paper-lined tray; refrigerate 30 minutes.
7 Heat vegetable oil in deep medium saucepan; deep-fry fritters, in batches, until browned lightly and heated through. Drain on absorbent paper. Serve fritters with a squeeze of lemon juice.

prep + cook time 1 hour 30 minutes (+ refrigeration)
makes 40
nutritional count per fritter 4.1g total fat (0.5g saturated fat); 379kJ (90 cal); 1.7g carbohydrate; 10.8g protein; 0.4g fibre
tip Salted cod, also known as salt cod, baccalà, bacalhau, bacalao and morue, is available from Spanish, Italian and Portuguese delicatessens and some speciality food stores. It needs to be de-salted and rehydrated before use.

pork ribs with chorizo & smoked paprika

1.5kg (3 pounds) american-style pork spareribs

4 cloves garlic, crushed

2 teaspoons smoked paprika

2 tablespoons olive oil

1 cured chorizo sausage (170g), sliced thinly

1 medium red onion (170g), chopped coarsely

1 medium red capsicum (bell pepper) (200g), chopped coarsely

1 tablespoon light brown sugar

800g (1½ pounds) canned chopped tomatoes

1 cup (250ml) chicken stock

¼ cup firmly packed fresh flat-leaf parsley leaves

1 Cut between bones of pork to separate into individual ribs. Combine garlic, paprika and half the olive oil in small bowl; rub over pork ribs.

2 Preheat oven to 160°C/325°F.

3 Cook chorizo in heated large flameproof baking dish, stirring, until browned lightly. Remove from dish with slotted spoon; drain on absorbent paper.

4 Cook ribs, in same dish, in batches, until browned. Drain on absorbent paper.

5 Add remaining oil, onion and capsicum to same dish; cook, stirring, until onion softens. Return ribs and chorizo to dish with sugar, undrained tomatoes and stock; bring to the boil.

6 Cover dish tightly with foil; cook, in oven, 1 hour. Remove foil; cook further 30 minutes or until ribs are tender. Season to taste. Serve ribs sprinkled with parsley.

prep + cook time 2 hours 15 minutes **serves** 4
nutritional count per serving 38.5g total fat (11.4g saturated fat); 2516kJ (602 cal); 15.6g carbohydrate; 49.2g protein; 4.1g fibre

grilled mussels with jamón

20 small black mussels (500g)

2 cups (500ml) water

80g (2½ ounces) butter, softened

50g (1½ ounces) thinly sliced jamón, chopped finely

1 clove garlic, crushed

2 green onions (scallions), chopped finely

1 Scrub mussels; remove beards. Bring the water to the boil in large saucepan. Add the mussels, cover; boil about 3 minutes or until mussels open.
2 Drain mussels; discard liquid. Break open shells; discard top shell. Loosen mussels from shells with a spoon; return mussels to shells, place in single layer on oven tray.
3 Preheat grill (broiler).
4 Combine butter, jamón, garlic and onion in small bowl. Divide butter mixture over mussels; grill about 3 minutes or until browned lightly.

prep + cook time 30 minutes **serves** 4
nutritional count per serving 17.6g total fat (11.2g saturated fat); 773kJ (185 cal); 1.8g carbohydrate; 5.5g protein; 0.2g fibre
tip Jamón is a type of Spanish cured ham, similar to prosciutto. It is available in specialty delicatessens. Use prosciutto if you can't get it.

MODERN MAINS We're spoilt for choice in Australian cities, in terms of ingredients and expertise from different cultures. Our favourite dishes often take inspiration from Mediterranean and Asian classics.

octopus in red wine

1.5kg (3 pounds) octopus tentacles

1½ cups (375ml) dry red wine

¼ cup (60ml) red wine vinegar

¼ cup (60ml) olive oil

2 cloves garlic, sliced thinly

2 bay leaves

1 fresh small red thai (serrano) chilli, sliced

1 cinnamon stick

2 teaspoons whole allspice

2 strips lemon rind

1½ cups (375ml) water

12 baby brown pickling onions (240g)

8 baby new potatoes (240g)

1 cup coarsely chopped fresh flat-leaf parsley

1 Preheat oven to 120°C/250°F.

2 Combine octopus, wine, vinegar, oil, garlic, bay leaves, chilli, cinnamon, allspice, rind and the water in large deep flameproof dish. Cook, covered, in oven 1 hour. Add onions to dish; cook, covered, further 30 minutes or until tender.

3 Remove octopus and onions from dish. Place dish on stovetop; bring liquid to the boil. Add potatoes; simmer, uncovered, about 20 minutes or until potatoes are tender. Remove potatoes, cut in half. Simmer sauce, uncovered, 15 minutes or until sauce is reduced to about 2 cups.

4 Meanwhile, thickly slice octopus.

5 Return octopus, onions and potatoes to sauce; cook until heated through. Just before serving, stir in parsley. Season to taste.

prep + cook time 2 hours 20 minutes **serves** 6
nutritional count per serving 11.7g total fat (2g saturated fat); 1421kJ (339 cal); 12.5g carbohydrate; 65.6g protein; 2.3g fibre
tip This recipe is suitable to freeze.

crisp-skinned fish
with roast garlic skordalia

4 x 200g (6½-ounce) white fish fillets, skin on

2 tablespoons plain (all-purpose) flour

ROAST GARLIC SKORDALIA

2 medium bulbs garlic (140g), unpeeled

600g (1¼ pounds) small potatoes

½ cup (125ml) milk, warmed

1 tablespoon finely grated lemon rind

½ cup (125ml) olive oil

½ cup (140g) Greek-style yogurt

¼ cup (60ml) lemon juice

ROSEMARY OIL

¼ cup (60ml) olive oil

4 cloves garlic, sliced thinly

2 tablespoons rosemary leaves

1 Make roast garlic skordalia.

2 Make rosemary oil.

3 Pat fish dry with absorbent paper; season. Sprinkle skin of fish with flour, rub in gently to cover skin completely; shake away excess flour.

4 Heat 1 tablespoon of the rosemary oil in medium frying pan; cook fish, skin-side down, about 2 minutes or until skin is crisp. Turn fish, cook fish through.

5 Serve fish with skordalia and drizzled with rosemary oil.

roast garlic skordalia Preheat oven to 220°C/425°F. Wrap garlic in foil; place on oven tray with potatoes. Roast about 30 minutes or until garlic and potatoes are soft. Stand until cool enough to handle. Peel potatoes; place flesh in medium bowl. Squeeze garlic from cloves, add to potatoes with half the warm milk. Mash rind, garlic and potatoes until smooth. Gradually stir in oil, 1 tablespoon at a time. Stir in yogurt and juice; season to taste. Just before serving, heat remaining milk in medium saucepan; add skordalia, cook, stirring, until heated through.

rosemary oil Heat oil, garlic and rosemary in small saucepan over low heat until garlic begins to colour. Cool.

prep + cook time 1 hour (+ cooling) **serves** 4
nutritional count per serving 53.4g total fat (11g saturated fat); 3210kJ (767 cal); 24g carbohydrate; 47.7g protein; 6.7g fibre
tip There are many recipes for skordalia – the roasted garlic gives this one a beautiful sweet and subtle taste.

seafood stew with fennel

2 baby fennel bulbs (260g)

2 tablespoons lemon juice

1 tablespoon olive oil

2 medium brown onions (300g), chopped finely

4 cloves garlic, crushed

1 orange

⅓ cup (80ml) dry white wine

1 teaspoon chilli flakes

pinch saffron threads

800g (1½ pounds) canned diced tomatoes

1 litre (4 cups) fish stock

1 teaspoon white (granulated) sugar

800g (1½ pounds) uncooked medium king prawns (shrimp)

800g (1½ pounds) small black mussels

750g (1½ pounds) skinless white fish fillets, cut into 3cm (1¼-inch) pieces

GARLIC CROUTONS

675g (1¼-pound) loaf sourdough bread, sliced thickly

3 cloves garlic, halved

2 tablespoons olive oil

1 Trim fennel; reserve feathery fronds. Slice fennel as thinly as possible; combine with lemon juice in small bowl.
2 Heat oil in large saucepan; cook onion, stirring, until soft. Add garlic; cook, stirring, 1 minute.
3 Peel three thin strips of rind from orange. Stir rind, wine, chilli and saffron into onion mixture; cook, stirring, 2 minutes. Add undrained tomatoes; simmer, uncovered, about 10 minutes or until mixture thickens slightly. Add stock; simmer, uncovered, about 20 minutes or until liquid is reduced by about a quarter. Stir in sugar.
4 Shell and devein prawns, leaving tails intact. Scrub mussels, remove beards.
5 Add prawns, mussels and fish to tomato mixture. Cover; simmer, stirring occasionally, about 5 minutes or until prawns change in colour and mussels open.
6 Meanwhile, make garlic croûtons.
7 Serve stew topped with garlic croûtons, fennel mixture and reserved fennel fronds.
garlic croûtons Toast bread both sides on heated grill plate (or grill or barbecue). Rub one side of toast with cut garlic clove; drizzle with oil.

prep + cook time 1 hour **serves** 6
nutritional count per serving 17.2g total fat (3.5g saturated fat); 2792kJ (668 cal); 63.7g carbohydrate; 56.9g protein; 9.2g fibre
tip You can buy the seafood already prepared from most fish markets; it will cost more, but will save you time.
serving suggestion Serve with a mixed leaf salad.

argentinean empanadas

2 tablespoons olive oil

750g (1½ pounds) beef chuck steak, chopped coarsely

1 medium brown onion (150g), chopped finely

2 teaspoons plain (all-purpose) flour

2 teaspoons ground cumin

1 teaspoon each ground coriander and sweet paprika

2 cups (500ml) beef stock

4 sheets shortcrust pastry

4 large green olives, seeded, sliced thinly

2 hard-boiled eggs, chopped coarsely

1 egg, beaten lightly

340g (11 ounces) bottled roasted capsicum (bell pepper) strips

1 Heat half the oil in large saucepan; cook beef, in batches, until browned. Remove from pan.
2 Heat remaining oil in same pan; cook onion, stirring, until softened. Add flour and spices; cook, stirring, 1 minute. Gradually stir in stock. Return beef to pan; bring to the boil. Reduce heat; simmer, covered, over low heat, 2 hours. Season; cool.
3 Preheat oven to 220°C/425°F. Oil oven tray and line with baking paper.
4 Cut eight 14cm (5½-inch) rounds from pastry. Divide beef mixture among rounds. Top with olive and hard-boiled egg; seal pastry over filling. Pinch pastry edges together; place on oven tray. Brush with beaten egg.
5 Bake empanadas about 25 minutes or until browned. Stand 5 minutes before serving.
6 Meanwhile, blend or process capsicum until smooth. Serve with empanadas.

prep + cook time 3 hours **makes** 8
nutritional count per empanada 36.7g total fat (15.7g saturated fat); 2587kJ (619 cal); 25.7g carbohydrate; 32.8g protein; 5.1g fibre
tip You can freeze the uncooked empanadas in an airtight container. No need to thaw them before baking but they will take a little longer.

goat's cheese

Made from goat's milk, goat's cheese has a distinctive tangy flavour. Good quality goat's cheese will have a citrus-flavoured tang, not an unpleasant goat taste that is sometimes associated with cheaper products.

The delicate balance of tartness and creaminess means that goat's cheese works well in many cuisines and in both savoury and sweet dishes. Goat's cheese is extremely versatile and can be used in soufflés, pizzas, salads and even some cakes. Australia produces a range of good-quality artisan goat's cheeses, predominantly in Western Australia, Victoria and New South Wales. The flavour is determined by the region, diet of the goats and the processing and aging of the cheese. There are two basic varieties of goat's cheese: fresh (unripened) and aged.

Fresh goat's cheese

Fresh, unripened goat's cheese, also called chèvre (the French word for goat), is pure white with a delicate tangy flavour. It is creamy and spreadable. Available in logs, pyramids and cones, fresh goat's cheese also comes rolled in ash or flavoured with herbs and spices. The ash protects the surface, and makes it an attractive addition to a cheese plate. Fresh goat's cheese is often marinated in olive oil with herbs and spices – the most common being garlic, chives, dill and peppercorns. It is also possible to buy fresh goat curd which is made by skimming the curd from the cheese vat within an hour of production and draining in cheesecloth.

Aged goat's cheese

The aged variety, while still pale in colour, is firmer with a more pronounced flavour. It is matured for at least four weeks and has a mottled, uneven rind.

Selecting goat's cheese

Fresh goat's cheese should be pure white and appear soft and moist. You can buy sealed goat's cheese in packages and jars from the supermarket or delicatessen, which is a good way to assure freshness. Always follow the use-by date on packaged goat's cheese.

Aged goat's cheese has a strong earthy (but not billy-goat) smell.

Nutritional content

Goat's cheese is lower in fat, calories and cholesterol than many cow's milk cheeses. It is also high in Vitamin A and potassium. The fats in goat's milk are easier to digest than those in cow's or sheep's milk, and for this reason, goat's cheese is a suitable option for people with a low tolerance for dairy.

Storing goat's cheese

Fresh, soft goat's cheese must be wrapped in plastic and kept in the refrigerator. Semi-hard aged cheeses should be wrapped first in baking paper and then loosely in plastic in order to allow the cheese to breathe without drying out. The wrapping must be changed regularly to maintain optimum freshness. Do not freeze goat's cheese.

slow-cooked tomato & goat's cheese tart

1kg (2 pounds) roma (egg) tomatoes, halved

2½ tablespoons extra virgin olive oil

⅓ cup small fresh basil leaves

1 sheet puff pastry

120g (4 ounces) fresh goat's cheese, at room temperature

1 Preheat oven to 120°C/250°F.

2 Toss tomatoes with 2 tablespoons of oil and ¼ cup of basil leaves in large bowl; season with salt and pepper. Place tomato mixture on a wire rack on an oven tray. Roast 3 hours, turning halfway through, until semi-dried. Discard dried basil leaves.

3 Increase oven to 220°C/425°F. Line oven tray with baking paper.

4 Place pastry on tray; mark a 1cm (½-inch) border around the edge with back of knife, prick inside border with fork. Bake 10 minutes; using a clean tea towel (to protect from steam), press down on centre of pastry. Bake another 7 minutes until pastry is golden and crisp.

5 Arrange tomatoes over pastry; crumble cheese on top. Drizzle with remaining oil; top with remaining basil.

prep + cook time 40 minutes **serves** 6
nutritional count per serving 17.2g total fat (3.6g saturated fat); 971kJ (232 cal); 13.4g carbohydrate; 5.9g protein; 2.5g fibre
tip You can roast the tomatoes in advance. Store in an airtight container in the fridge. To reheat, place them on an oven tray and return to the oven when baking the pastry for 5-6 minutes until warm.

duck confit with pan-fried kipflers & pear watercress salad

2 x 2kg (4-pound) whole ducks

1 tablespoon coarse cooking (kosher) salt

2 cloves garlic, sliced thinly

1 bay leaf, crumbled

2 sprigs fresh thyme

2 teaspoons black peppercorns

2 cups (500ml) olive oil

750g (1½ pounds) kipfler (fingerling) potatoes, halved lengthways

PEAR WATERCRESS SALAD

1 tablespoon wholegrain mustard

1 tablespoon white wine vinegar

1 teaspoon white (granulated) sugar

¼ cup (60ml) olive oil

3 cups (350g) firmly packed trimmed watercress

1 large pear (330g), sliced thinly

1 Using sharp knife, cut marylands and breasts off ducks. Remove as much fat as possible from carcasses; reserve. Discard wings and carcasses.
2 Combine duck pieces, salt, garlic, bay leaf, thyme and peppercorns in medium bowl. Cover; refrigerate until required.
3 Meanwhile, place reserved fat in large saucepan; cook, uncovered, over low heat, about 1 hour or until fat has melted. Strain mixture through fine sieve into large bowl; discard solids (you will have about 2 cups of duck fat).

4 Preheat oven to 150°C/300°F.
5 Rinse duck pieces under cold water; pat dry with absorbent paper. Place duck pieces, in single layer, in large baking dish. Reserve 2 tablespoons of the fat; pour remaining fat over duck. Top up with olive oil, making sure duck is completely submerged. Roast, uncovered, 2 hours.
6 Boil, steam or microwave potatoes until tender; drain. Heat reserved fat in large frying pan; cook potato, in batches, until browned. Remove from pan; cover to keep warm.
7 Meanwhile, make pear watercress salad.
8 Place duck in same large frying pan; cook, skin-side down, until skin is crisp. Serve duck with potato and salad.
pear watercress salad Place mustard, vinegar, sugar and oil in screw-top jar; shake well. Place watercress and pear in large bowl with dressing; toss gently to combine.

prep + cook time 4 hours **serves** 6
nutritional count per serving 184.2g total fat (41.6g saturated fat); 8628kJ (2064 cal); 24.5g carbohydrate; 79.9g protein; 5.5g fibre
tips Duck carcasses and wings can be used to make stock. Cooked duck can be stored up to 1 month, completely covered in fat, in tightly sealed glass container, in the refrigerator. To reheat duck, remove from fat, wrap in foil and place in 120°C/250°F oven for about 30 minutes.

chicken & artichoke fricassee

2 tablespoons olive oil

8 chicken drumsticks (1.2kg)

1 medium brown onion (150g), chopped finely

4 cloves garlic, crushed

½ cup (125ml) dry white wine

1½ cups (375ml) chicken stock

1 tablespoon finely grated lemon rind

1 tablespoon lemon juice

1¼ cups (310ml) pouring cream

125g (4 ounces) baby spinach leaves

680g (1¼ pounds) canned marinated artichokes in oil, drained, halved

1 tablespoon finely chopped fresh oregano

1 tablespoon fresh oregano leaves

1 Heat half the oil in large saucepan; cook chicken, in batches, until browned. Remove from pan.
2 Heat remaining oil in same pan; cook onion and garlic, stirring, until onion softens. Add wine, stock, rind and juice; bring to the boil. Return chicken to pan; reduce heat, simmer, covered, 20 minutes. Uncover; simmer, about 10 minutes or until chicken is cooked through.
3 Remove chicken from pan, place two drumsticks in each serving bowl.
4 Combine cream, spinach, artichokes and chopped oregano in pan with sauce mixture; bring to the boil. Reduce heat; simmer, uncovered, about 2 minutes or until sauce thickens slightly. Pour sauce over chicken; sprinkle with oregano leaves.

prep + cook time 1 hour 10 minutes **serves** 4
nutritional count per serving 65.4g total fat (29.8g saturated fat); 3315kJ (793 cal); 7.4g carbohydrate; 39.4g protein; 2g fibre
tip It is fine to use just one 300ml carton of cream for this recipe.
serving suggestion Serve with steamed white rice.

boeuf bourguignon

280g (9 ounces) baby brown onions

2 tablespoons olive oil

2kg (4 pounds) gravy beef, trimmed, chopped

30g (1 ounce) butter

2 cloves garlic, crushed

4 rindless bacon slices (260g), chopped coarsely

400g (13 ounces) button mushrooms, halved

¼ cup (35g) plain (all-purpose) flour

1¼ cups (310ml) beef stock

2½ cups (625ml) dry red wine

2 bay leaves

2 sprigs fresh thyme

½ cup coarsely chopped fresh flat-leaf parsley

1 Peel onions, leaving root end intact so onion remains whole during cooking.

2 Heat oil in large flameproof dish; cook beef, over heat, in batches, until browned. Remove from pan.

3 Add butter to dish; cook onions, garlic, bacon and mushrooms, stirring, until onions brown lightly.

4 Sprinkle flour over onion mixture; cook, stirring, until flour mixture thickens and bubbles. Gradually add stock and wine; stir over heat until mixture boils and thickens.

5 Return beef and any juices to dish, add bay leaves and thyme; bring to the boil. Reduce heat; simmer, covered, about 2 hours or until beef is tender, stirring every 30 minutes. Remove from heat; discard bay leaves. Stir in parsley.

prep + cook time 2 hours 45 minutes **serves** 6
nutritional count per serving 31.4g total fat
(12.1g saturated fat); 2658kJ (636 cal);
6.6g carbohydrate; 80.3g protein; 2.8g fibre

Melbourne, Victoria

coq au vin

750g (1½ pounds) spring onions

¼ cup (60ml) olive oil

6 rindless bacon slices (390g), chopped coarsely

310g (10½ ounces) button mushrooms

2 cloves garlic, crushed

8 chicken thigh fillets (880g)

¼ cup (35g) plain (all-purpose) flour

2 cups (500ml) dry red wine

1½ cups (375ml) chicken stock

2 tablespoons tomato paste

3 bay leaves

4 sprigs fresh thyme

2 sprigs fresh rosemary

1 Trim green ends from onions, leaving about 4cm (1½ inches) of stem attached; trim roots.

2 Heat 1 tablespoon of the oil in large frying pan; cook onions, stirring, until browned all over. Remove from pan.

3 Cook bacon, mushrooms and garlic in same pan, stirring, until bacon is crisp. Remove from pan.

4 Coat chicken in flour; shake off excess. Heat remaining oil in same pan; cook chicken, in batches, until browned all over. Remove from pan; drain on absorbent paper.

5 Return chicken to pan with wine, stock, paste, bay leaves, herbs, onions and bacon mixture. Bring to the boil; reduce heat, simmer, uncovered, about 35 minutes or until chicken is tender and sauce has thickened slightly.

prep + cook time 1 hour 30 minutes **serves** 4
nutritional count per serving 43.6g total fat
(11.8g saturated fat); 3428kJ (820 cal);
16.3g carbohydrate; 67.8g protein; 6.4g fibre

braised beef cheeks in red wine

2 tablespoons olive oil

1.6kg (3¼ pounds) beef cheeks, trimmed

1 medium brown onion (150g), chopped coarsely

1 medium carrot (120g), chopped coarsely

3 cups (750ml) dry red wine

¼ cup (60ml) red wine vinegar

800g (1½ pounds) canned whole tomatoes

¼ cup (55g) firmly packed light brown sugar

2 sprigs fresh rosemary

6 black peppercorns

2 tablespoons fresh oregano leaves

1 large fennel bulb (550g), cut into thin wedges

400g (12½ ounces) spring onions, trimmed, halved

200g (6½ ounces) swiss brown mushrooms

1 Preheat oven to 160°C/325°F.

2 Heat half the oil in large flameproof dish; cook beef, over heat, in batches, until browned. Remove from dish.

3 Heat remaining oil in same dish; cook brown onion and carrot, stirring, until onion softens. Return beef to dish with wine, vinegar, undrained tomatoes, sugar, rosemary, peppercorns, oregano and fennel; bring to the boil. Cover dish, transfer to oven; roast 2 hours.

4 Stir in spring onions and mushrooms; roast, uncovered, 45 minutes or until beef is tender.

prep + cook time 3 hours 30 minutes **serves** 4
nutritional count per serving 41.6g total fat (14.9g saturated fat); 4188kJ (1002 cal); 30.9g carbohydrate; 90.2g protein; 9.6g fibre
serving suggestion Serve with soft polenta.

osso buco

6 pieces veal osso buco (1.8kg)

½ cup (75g) plain (all-purpose) flour

40g (1½ ounces) butter

2 tablespoons olive oil

3 sticks celery (450g), trimmed, chopped coarsely

6 drained anchovy fillets, chopped coarsely

¾ cup (180ml) dry white wine

800g (1½ pounds) canned diced tomatoes

½ cup (125ml) chicken stock

5 cloves garlic, crushed

10 fresh thyme sprigs

3 bay leaves

GREMOLATA

½ cup finely chopped fresh flat-leaf parsley

2 cloves garlic, chopped finely

1 teaspoon finely grated lemon rind

1 Preheat oven to 160°C/325°F.

2 Coat veal in flour, shake off any excess. Heat butter and oil in large frying pan; cook veal, in batches, until browned both sides. Transfer veal to large ovenproof dish.

3 Cook celery and anchovy in same pan, stirring, until celery softens. Add wine; bring to the boil. Stir in undrained tomatoes, stock, garlic, thyme and bay leaves; return to the boil.

4 Pour tomato mixture over veal; cook, covered, in oven about 1½ hours or until veal starts to fall away from the bone.

5 Meanwhile, make gremolata.

6 Serve osso buco sprinkled with gremolata.

gremolata Combine ingredients in small bowl.

prep + cook time 2 hours **serves** 6

nutritional count per serving 13.2g total fat (4.8g saturated fat); 1626kJ (389 cal); 14.4g carbohydrate; 46.1g protein; 3.8g fibre

tip Osso buco originates from Milan and is traditionally served on risotto alla milanese (saffron risotto) with a good sprinkle of gremolata. Here we've served it on polenta.

rabbit stew

2 tablespoons oil

1kg (2 pounds) rabbit pieces

3 medium brown onions (450g), sliced thickly

4 cloves garlic, crushed

1 cup (250ml) water

1 litre (4 cups) chicken stock

410g (13 ounces) canned diced tomatoes

5 medium potatoes (1kg), chopped coarsely

2 medium carrots (240g), sliced thickly

1 tablespoon balsamic vinegar

3 bay leaves

1 teaspoon dried chilli flakes

⅓ cup coarsely chopped fresh mint

1 cup (120g) frozen peas

1 Heat half the oil in large saucepan; cook rabbit, in batches, until browned. Remove from pan.
2 Heat remaining oil in same pan; cook onion and garlic, stirring, until onion softens.
3 Add the water, stock, undrained tomatoes, potato, carrot, vinegar, bay leaves, chilli and mint to pan. Return rabbit to pan; bring to the boil. Reduce heat; simmer, uncovered, 1¼ hours. Add peas; simmer, uncovered, 5 minutes.

prep + cook time 2 hours 5 minutes **serves** 4
nutritional count per serving 19.4g total fat (5.1g saturated fat); 2750kJ (658 cal); 44.4g carbohydrate; 70.7g protein; 10.6g fibre

Melbourne, Victoria

slow-roasted lamb shanks with caramelised onion

1 tablespoon olive oil

8 french-trimmed lamb shanks (2kg)

1 tablespoon white (granulated) sugar

1½ cups (375ml) dry red wine

2 cups (500ml) beef stock

3 cloves garlic, crushed

20g (¾ ounce) butter

1 small brown onion (80g), chopped finely

1 stick celery (150g), trimmed, chopped finely

1 tablespoon plain (all-purpose) flour

1 tablespoon tomato paste

1 tablespoon coarsely chopped fresh rosemary

CARAMELISED ONION

40g (1½ ounces) butter

2 medium red onions (340g), sliced thinly

¼ cup (55g) firmly packed light brown sugar

¼ cup (60ml) raspberry vinegar

1 Preheat oven to 150°C/300°F.

2 Heat oil in large flameproof dish; cook lamb until browned all over. Stir in sugar, wine, stock and garlic; bring to the boil. Cover dish, transfer to oven; roast lamb about 4 hours, turning twice during cooking.

3 Meanwhile, make caramelised onion.

4 Remove lamb from dish; cover to keep warm. Pour pan juices into large heatproof jug. Return dish to heat, melt butter; cook onion and celery, stirring, until celery is just tender. Stir in flour; cook, stirring, 2 minutes. Add reserved pan juices, paste and rosemary; bring to the boil. Reduce heat; simmer, uncovered, stirring, about 10 minutes or until mixture boils and thickens; strain sauce into large heatproof jug.

5 Serve lamb with sauce and caramelised onion.

caramelised onion Melt butter in medium saucepan; cook onion, stirring, about 15 minutes or until browned and soft. Stir in sugar and vinegar; cook, stirring, about 15 minutes or until onion has caramelised.

prep + cook time 4 hours 50 minutes **serves** 4
nutritional count per serving 41.8g total fat (20.1g saturated fat); 3298kJ (789 cal); 27.3g carbohydrate; 59.8g protein; 2.4g fibre
serving suggestion Serve on white bean puree or mashed potato.

lamb shanks with lentils

1 tablespoon olive oil

6 french-trimmed lamb shanks (1.5kg)

1 large brown onion (200g), chopped finely

2 sticks celery (300g), trimmed, chopped finely

1 medium carrot (120g), sliced finely

2 bay leaves

3 cups (750ml) chicken stock

1 cup (250ml) water

1¼ cups (250g) dried brown lentils, rinsed

2 tablespoons lemon juice

2 tablespoons coarsely chopped
fresh flat-leaf parsley

1 Heat oil in large saucepan; cook lamb, in batches, until browned. Remove from pan.
2 Add onion, celery, carrot and bay leaves to pan; cook, stirring, 5 minutes or until onion softens.
3 Return lamb to pan with stock and the water; bring to the boil. Reduce heat; simmer, covered, 1 hour. Stir in lentils; bring to the boil. Reduce heat; simmer, covered, 30 minutes. Uncover; simmer further 30 minutes or until lamb and lentils are tender.
4 Stir in juice and parsley; season to taste.

prep + cook time 2 hours 30 minutes **serves** 6
nutritional count per serving 12.1g total fat (4.3g saturated fat); 1547kJ (370 cal); 20.8g carbohydrate; 41.5g protein; 7.4g fibre
tip You could use lamb leg or shoulder, cut into chunks, instead of shanks.
serving suggestion Serve with a rocket salad.

slow-cooked lamb with white beans

1¼ cups (250g) dried cannellini beans

18 shallots (450g)

1 medium orange (240g), sliced thinly

3 cloves garlic, chopped coarsely

3 bay leaves

10 sprigs fresh thyme

½ teaspoon black peppercorns

1 bottle (750ml) dry red wine

2 x 1kg (2-pound) lamb shoulders

1 tablespoon olive oil

3 sticks celery (450g), trimmed, cut into 4cm (1½-inch) lengths

½ cup (95g) tomato paste

750g (1½ pounds) pumpkin, trimmed, cut into 3cm (1¼-inch) cubes

½ cup finely chopped fresh flat-leaf parsley

1 Place beans in medium bowl, cover with water; stand overnight. Combine shallots, orange, garlic, bay leaves, thyme, peppercorns, wine and lamb in large dish. Cover; refrigerate overnight.
2 Rinse beans; drain. Place in large saucepan of boiling water; return to the boil. Reduce heat; simmer, uncovered, about 15 minutes or until beans are just tender.
3 Preheat oven to 160°C/325°F.
4 Meanwhile, heat oil in large flameproof dish on stove top. Drain lamb, reserve marinade. Brown one lamb shoulder at a time in dish.
5 Add unstrained marinade to dish with celery and beans; bring to the boil. Add lamb to dish; transfer to oven. Cook, covered, about 2 hours or until lamb starts to fall from the bones. Remove lamb from dish; cover to keep warm.
6 Stir paste and pumpkin into dish, simmer, uncovered, on stove top about 15 minutes or until pumpkin is tender.
7 Serve sliced lamb with bean mixture; sprinkle with parsley and, if you like, a little thinly sliced lemon rind.

prep + cook time 3 hours (+ standing & refrigeration)
serves 6
nutritional count per serving 26.6g total fat (11g saturated fat); 2976kJ (712 cal); 29.8g carbohydrate; 61.5g protein; 12.3g fibre
tips If you don't have time to soak the dried beans overnight, you can use three 400g (12½-ounce) cans cannellini beans, rinsed and drained. Add them to the dish after 1 hour of cooking time. If you want to top the lamb with lemon strips, use a zester or peel the rind from a lemon into long strips, cut away all the white pith, then slice rind finely.

creamy mushroom & spinach gnocchi

625g (1¼ pounds) fresh potato gnocchi

375g (12 ounces) assorted mushrooms, sliced thinly

2 cloves garlic, crushed

1¼ cups (310ml) pouring cream

90g (3 ounces) baby spinach leaves

⅓ cup (25g) finely grated parmesan cheese

1 Cook gnocchi in large saucepan of boiling water until tender; drain.

2 Meanwhile, cook mushrooms and garlic in heated oiled large frying pan, stirring, until softened. Add cream and spinach; bring to the boil. Reduce heat; simmer, uncovered, until spinach wilts and sauce thickens. Stir in half the cheese. Season to taste.

3 Add gnocchi to pan, stir gently. Serve gnocchi topped with remaining cheese.

prep + cook time 10 minutes **serves** 4
nutritional count per serving 36.2g total fat
(23.4g saturated fat); 2458kJ (588 cal);
48.2g carbohydrate; 14.4g protein; 6.8g fibre
tips It is fine to use just one 300ml carton of cream for this recipe. Try using a variety of mushrooms such as button, flat, cup and portobello.

prawn & scallop tortellini

500g (1 pound) uncooked medium king prawns (shrimp)

250g (8 ounces) scallops without roe

1 tablespoon olive oil

2 tablespoons each finely chopped fresh vietnamese mint and chervil

2 tablespoons finely chopped preserved lemon rind

220g (7 ounces) soft goat's cheese

2 teaspoons sea salt

1 teaspoon cracked black pepper

275g (9 ounces) round gow gee wrappers

LEMON DRESSING

¼ cup (60ml) lemon juice

½ cup (125ml) olive oil

1 tablespoon each finely chopped fresh chervil and flat-leaf parsley

1 Make lemon dressing.

2 Shell and devein prawns. Coarsely chop prawn meat and scallops. Heat oil in large frying pan; cook seafood over medium heat until prawns change colour. Cool.

3 Combine seafood, herbs, rind, cheese, salt and pepper in medium bowl.

4 To make tortellini, place a gow gee wrapper on bench; place 1 level tablespoon of the seafood mixture in centre, brush edge with water. Fold in half; bring two points together, to make a crescent shape, press gently to seal. Repeat with remaining wrappers and filling.

5 Cook tortellini in large saucepan of boiling water until tortellini float to the top; drain. Transfer tortellini to large heatproof bowl; drizzle with a little dressing.

6 Serve tortellini drizzled with remaining dressing; sprinkle with extra chervil sprigs.

lemon dressing Place ingredients in screw-top jar; shake well.

prep + cook time 40 minutes (+ standing) **serves** 6
nutritional count per serving 15g total fat
(6.3g saturated fat); 1500kJ (358 cal);
27.3g carbohydrate; 27.6g protein; 0.4g fibre
tips Cover gow gee wrappers with a damp tea towel to stop them drying out while making the tortellini. The tortellini can be made a day ahead; store, in a single layer, covered in plastic wrap, in the refrigerator until ready to cook. Preserved lemons are available from delis and some supermarkets. Bear in mind that only the rind is used in cooking, so discard the flesh from each piece first. Rinse the rind well before chopping finely.

spinach & ricotta cannelloni

1kg (2 pounds) spinach, trimmed, chopped coarsely

500g (1 pound) ricotta cheese

2 eggs

¼ cup finely chopped fresh mint

3 teaspoons finely chopped fresh thyme

2 teaspoons finely chopped fresh rosemary

1½ cups (120g) coarsely grated parmesan cheese

250g (8 ounces) cannelloni tubes

CREAMY TOMATO SAUCE

1 tablespoon olive oil

1 medium brown onion (150g), chopped finely

4 cloves garlic, crushed

4 x 400g (12½ ounces) canned diced tomatoes

½ cup (125ml) pouring cream

1 teaspoon white (granulated) sugar

1 Make creamy tomato sauce.

2 Meanwhile, preheat oven to 180°C/350°F.

3 Cook washed, drained (not dried) spinach in heated large saucepan, stirring, until wilted. Drain; when cool enough to handle, squeeze out excess moisture.

4 Combine spinach in large bowl with ricotta, eggs, herbs and ½ cup of the parmesan. Spoon mixture into a large piping bag; pipe into cannelloni tubes.

5 Spread a third of the tomato sauce into shallow 25cm x 35cm (10¼-inch x 14-inch) ovenproof dish; top with cannelloni tubes, in single layer, then top with remaining sauce.

6 Bake cannelloni, covered, 20 minutes. Uncover, sprinkle with remaining parmesan; cook further 15 minutes or until pasta is tender and cheese is browned lightly.

creamy tomato sauce Heat oil in large saucepan; cook onion, stirring, until softened. Add garlic; cook, stirring, until fragrant. Add undrained tomatoes; bring to the boil. Reduce heat; simmer, uncovered, stirring occasionally, about 20 minutes or until sauce thickens slightly. Cool 10 minutes; blend or process sauce with cream and sugar until smooth.

prep + cook time 1 hour **serves** 6
nutritional count per serving 31g total fat (17.1g saturated fat); 2412kJ (577 cal); 41.8g carbohydrate; 28.7g protein; 8.3g fibre
tip The cannelloni can be prepared completely up to a day ahead, ready to go into the oven. Keep it covered in the refrigerator overnight.

prawn & asparagus risotto

500g (1 pound) uncooked medium
king prawns (shrimp)

3 cups (750ml) chicken stock

3 cups (750ml) water

15g (½ ounce) butter

1 tablespoon olive oil

1 small brown onion (80g), chopped finely

2 cups (400g) arborio rice

½ cup (125ml) dry sherry

15g (½ ounce) butter, extra

2 teaspoons olive oil, extra

2 cloves garlic, crushed

500g (1 pound) asparagus, chopped coarsely

⅓ cup (25g) coarsely grated parmesan cheese

⅓ cup loosely packed fresh basil leaves

1 Shell and devein prawns, leaving tails intact.
2 Place stock and the water in large saucepan; bring to the boil. Reduce heat; simmer, covered.
3 Meanwhile, heat butter and oil in large saucepan; cook onion, stirring, until soft. Add rice; stir to coat rice in onion mixture. Add sherry; cook, stirring, until liquid is almost evaporated.
4 Stir in 1 cup simmering stock mixture; cook, stirring, over low heat until liquid is absorbed. Continue adding stock mixture, in 1-cup batches, stirring, until absorbed after each addition. Total cooking time should be about 35 minutes or until rice is tender.
5 Heat extra butter and extra oil in medium frying pan; cook prawns and garlic, stirring, until prawns just change colour.
6 Meanwhile, boil, steam or microwave asparagus until just tender; drain.
7 Add asparagus, prawn mixture and cheese to risotto; cook, stirring, until cheese melts. Serve risotto sprinkled with basil.

prep + cook time 1 hour 10 minutes **serves** 4
nutritional count per serving 14.7g total fat
(5.5g saturated fat); 2516kJ (602 cal);
82.8g carbohydrate; 26.3g protein; 2.6g fibre

Melbourne, Victoria

porterhouse steaks
with blue cheese mash

1 tablespoon olive oil

20g (¾ ounce) butter

2 large red onions (600g), sliced thinly

2 tablespoons light brown sugar

2 tablespoons balsamic vinegar

4 porterhouse steaks (1kg)

½ cup (125ml) dry red wine

¾ cup (180ml) chicken stock

20g (¾ ounce) cold butter, chopped, extra

BLUE CHEESE MASH

1kg (2 pounds) coliban potatoes, chopped coarsely

40g (1½ ounces) butter, softened

¾ cup (180ml) hot milk

100g (3 ounces) firm blue cheese, crumbled

¼ cup coarsely chopped fresh chives

1 Heat oil and butter in large frying pan; cook onion, stirring, until softened. Add sugar and vinegar; cook, stirring occasionally, about 15 minutes or until onion caramelises. Cover to keep warm.

2 Meanwhile, make blue cheese mash.

3 Cook steaks, in batches, in large heated lightly oiled frying pan until cooked as desired. Cover steaks; stand 10 minutes.

4 Meanwhile, bring wine to the boil in same frying pan; boil, uncovered, until reduced by half. Add stock; return to the boil. Whisk in cold butter, piece by piece, until sauce is smooth.

5 Divide mash, steaks and onion among serving plates; drizzle with sauce.

blue cheese mash Boil, steam or microwave potato until tender, drain. Mash potato in large bowl with butter and milk until smooth; fold in cheese and chives. Cover to keep warm.

prep + cook time 1 hour 10 minutes **serves** 4
nutritional count per serving 54.1g total fat (28.1g saturated fat); 3958kJ (947 cal); 43.3g carbohydrate; 66.6g protein; 5.5g fibre
tip The blue cheeses of England, France and Italy, stilton, roquefort and gorgonzola, respectively, are the mould-ripened cheese copied by other countries when making savoury, aromatic, firm blue-vein cheeses. These are the best blues to cook with, as their distinctive flavour doesn't dissipate when introduced to heat.

aromatic vietnamese beef curry

2 tablespoons peanut oil

750g (1½ pounds) beef strips

1 medium brown onion (150g), chopped finely

3 cloves garlic, crushed

1 fresh long red chilli, chopped finely

10cm (4-inch) stick fresh lemon grass (20g), chopped finely

1 star anise

1 cinnamon stick

4 cardamom pods, bruised

375g (12 ounces) snake beans, cut into 4cm (1½-inch) lengths

2 tablespoons ground bean sauce

2 tablespoons fish sauce

½ cup coarsely chopped fresh coriander (cilantro)

½ cup (40g) flaked almonds, roasted

1 Heat half the oil in wok; stir-fry beef, in batches, until browned. Remove from wok; cover to keep warm.

2 Heat remaining oil in wok; stir-fry onion until soft. Add garlic, chilli, lemon grass, star anise, cinnamon, cardamom and beans; stir-fry until beans are tender.

3 Return beef to wok with sauces; stir-fry until heated through. Stir in coriander and nuts off the heat. Discard star anise, cinnamon and cardamom before serving.

prep + cook time 35 minutes **serves** 4
nutritional count per serving 27.2g total fat (7.1g saturated fat); 2011kJ (481 cal); 7.4g carbohydrate; 49.6g protein; 4.9g fibre
tip You can thinly slice rump or scotch fillet steaks instead of using beef strips.

pho bo

1kg (2 pounds) beef chuck steak

2 star anise

8cm (3¼-inch) piece fresh ginger (40g), grated

⅓ cup (80ml) japanese soy sauce

2 litres (8 cups) water

1 litre (4 cups) beef stock

200g (6½ ounces) bean thread noodles

1½ cups (120g) bean sprouts

¼ cup loosely packed fresh coriander (cilantro) leaves

⅓ cup loosely packed fresh mint leaves

4 green onions (scallions), sliced thinly

2 fresh long red chillies, sliced thinly

¼ cup (60ml) fish sauce

1 lime

1 Place beef, star anise, ginger and soy sauce in large suacepan with the water and stock; bring to the boil. Reduce heat; simmer, covered, 30 minutes. Uncover; simmer about 30 minutes or until beef is tender.

2 Meanwhile, place noodles in medium heatproof bowl, cover with boiling water; stand until just tender, drain.

3 Combine sprouts, herbs, onion and chilli in medium bowl.

4 Remove beef from pan. Strain broth through muslin-lined sieve or colander into large heatproof bowl; discard solids. When beef is cool enough to handle, remove and discard fat and sinew. Slice beef thinly, return to same cleaned pan with broth; bring to the boil. Stir in fish sauce.

5 Divide noodles among bowls; ladle hot beef broth into bowls, sprinkle with sprout mixture and serve with lime cheeks.

prep + cook time 1 hour 40 minutes **serves** 6
nutritional count per serving 13.8g total fat (6.2g saturated fat); 1601kJ (383 cal); 21g carbohydrate; 41.3g protein; 4.1g fibre
tips Large bowls of pho (noodle soup) are a breakfast favourite throughout Vietnam, but we like to eat it any time of the day. Round steak, gravy beef (shin) and skirt steak are all suitable for this recipe.

thai green prawn curry

2 tablespoons green curry paste

500g (1 pound) uncooked shelled medium king prawns (shrimp), tails intact

150g (4½ ounces) snow peas, trimmed, halved

500g (1 pound) gai lan, cut into 5cm (2-inch) lengths

2 teaspoons fish sauce

1⅔ cups (410ml) coconut milk

½ cup (125ml) water

¼ cup loosely packed fresh thai basil leaves

1 Cook curry paste in heated large deep frying pan, stirring, until fragrant.
2 Add prawns, peas, gai lan, sauce, coconut milk and the water to pan; bring to the boil, stirring. Reduce heat; simmer, uncovered, about 5 minutes or until prawns change colour and sauce thickens. Season to taste.
3 Serve curry sprinkled with thai basil.

prep + cook time 10 minutes **serves** 4
nutritional count per serving 25.4g total fat (18.6g saturated fat); 1639kJ (392 cal); 7.8g carbohydrate; 30.9g protein; 5.4g fibre
serving suggestion Serve with steamed jasmine rice.

pad thai

40g (1½ ounces) tamarind pulp

½ cup (125ml) boiling water

2 tablespoons grated palm sugar

⅓ cup (80ml) sweet chilli sauce

⅓ cup (80ml) fish sauce

375g (12 ounces) rice stick noodles

12 uncooked medium prawns (shrimp) (500g)

2 cloves garlic, crushed

2 tablespoons finely chopped preserved turnip

2 tablespoons dried shrimp

4cm (1½-inch) piece fresh ginger (20g), grated

2 fresh small red thai (serrano) chillies, chopped coarsely

1 tablespoon peanut oil

250g (8 ounces) minced (ground) pork

3 eggs, beaten lightly

2 cups (160g) bean sprouts

4 green onions (scallions), sliced thinly

⅓ cup coarsely chopped fresh coriander (cilantro)

¼ cup (35g) coarsely chopped roasted unsalted peanuts

1 lime, quartered

1 Soak tamarind pulp in the boiling water for 30 minutes. Pour tamarind mixture into fine strainer over small bowl; push as much tamarind pulp through strainer as possible, scraping underside of strainer occasionally. Discard any tamarind solids left in strainer; reserve pulp liquid in bowl. Stir sugar and sauces into pulp liquid.

2 Meanwhile, place noodles in large heatproof bowl; cover with boiling water. Stand until just tender; drain.

3 Shell and devein prawns, leaving tails intact.

4 Blend or process garlic, turnip, shrimp, ginger and chilli until mixture forms a paste.

5 Heat oil in wok; stir-fry garlic paste until fragrant. Add pork; stir-fry until just cooked through. Add prawns; stir-fry 1 minute. Add egg; stir-fry until egg just sets. Add noodles, tamarind mixture, sprouts and half of the onion; stir-fry, tossing gently until combined. Remove from heat; add remaining green onion, coriander and nuts, toss gently until combined. Serve with lime wedges.

prep + cook time 40 minutes (+ standing) serves 4
nutritional count per serving 19.7g total fat (4.5g saturated fat); 2608kJ (624 cal); 65.6g carbohydrate; 42.6g protein; 5.4g fibre
tip Preserved turnip is also called hua chai po or cu cai muoi, or dried radish because of its similarity to daikon. Sold packaged whole or sliced, it is very salty and must be rinsed and dried before use.

sweet & soy pork

500g (1 pound) fresh wide rice noodles

1½ tablespoons peanut oil

500g (1 pound) pork fillet, sliced thinly

300g (9½ ounces) gai lan, chopped coarsely

3 cloves garlic, crushed

2 tablespoons each light soy sauce and
dark soy sauce

2 tablespoons light brown sugar

1 egg

1 Place noodles in large heatproof bowl, cover with boiling water; separate with fork, drain.
2 Heat 1 tablespoon of the oil in wok; stir-fry pork, in batches, until browned. Remove from wok.
3 Separate leaves and stems from gai lan. Heat remaining oil in wok; stir-fry gai lan stems until tender. Add gai lan leaves and garlic; stir-fry until gai lan wilts. Return pork to wok with noodles, sauces and sugar; stir-fry until hot.
4 Make a well in centre of noodles, add egg; stir-fry egg until egg and noodle mixture are combined, season to taste.

prep + cook time 20 minutes **serves** 4
nutritional count per serving 12g total fat
(2.7g saturated fat); 1622kJ (388 cal);
34.6g carbohydrate; 34g protein; 2.2g fibre
tip Traditionally, this recipe is known as pork pad see ew.
serving suggestion Serve topped with finely sliced fresh red chilli.

char kway teow

450g (14½ ounces) wide fresh rice noodles

250g (8 ounces) uncooked small prawns (shrimp)

250g (8 ounces) squid hoods

⅓ cup (80ml) peanut oil

250g (8 ounces) firm white fish fillets, skinned, cut into 3cm (1¼-inch) pieces

2 cloves garlic, crushed

2 fresh small red thai (serrano) chillies, chopped finely

4cm (1½-inch) piece fresh ginger (20g), grated

2 eggs, beaten lightly

5 green onions (scallions), sliced thinly

2 cups (160g) bean sprouts

120g (4 ounces) dried chinese sausage, sliced thinly

2 tablespoons dark soy sauce

1 tablespoon each kecap manis and light soy sauce

1 Place noodles in large heatproof bowl; cover with boiling water, separate with fork, drain.
2 Shell and devein prawns, leaving tails intact. Cut squid down centre to open out; score inside in diagonal pattern, then cut into 2cm (¾-inch) wide strips.
3 Heat 1 tablespoon of the oil in wok; stir-fry fish and squid, in batches, until browned lightly. Place in large bowl; cover to keep warm.
4 Heat another tablespoon of the oil in wok; stir-fry prawns, garlic, chilli and ginger until prawns just change colour. Add to bowl with fish and squid; cover to keep warm.
5 Heat remaining oil in wok; stir-fry egg, onion and sprouts until egg is just set. Slide egg mixture onto plate; cover to keep warm.
6 Stir-fry sausage in wok until crisp; drain. Return sausage to wok with seafood, egg mixture, sauces and noodles; stir-fry until hot.

prep + cook time 35 minutes **serves** 4
nutritional count per serving 29.9g total fat (6.9g saturated fat); 2291kJ (548 cal); 27g carbohydrate; 41.1g protein; 3.3g fibre
tip Dried chinese sausages, also called lap cheong, are usually made from pork but can also be made with duck liver or beef. Red-brown in colour and sweet-spicy in flavour, the 12cm (4¾-inch) dried links are sold, several strung together, in supermarkets.

lamb with snake beans

1½ cups (300g) jasmine rice

1 tablespoon peanut oil

2 shallots (50g), sliced thinly

2 cloves garlic, crushed

3cm (1¼-inch) piece fresh ginger (15g), grated

1 fresh small red thai (serrano) chilli, sliced thinly

500g (1 pound) minced (ground) lamb

1 cup (250ml) chicken stock

2 tablespoons fish sauce

1½ tablespoons grated palm sugar

2 teaspoons finely grated lime rind

315g (10 ounces) snake beans, chopped coarsely

2 tablespoons lime juice

1 cup each loosely packed fresh coriander (cilantro) and thai basil leaves

1 lime, extra, cut into wedges

1 Cook rice according to packet directions; cover to keep warm.
2 Meanwhile, heat wok over high heat, add oil; stir-fry shallots, garlic, ginger and chilli until fragrant. Add lamb; stir-fry until browned.
3 Stir in stock, sauce, sugar and rind; bring to the boil. Add beans; stir until tender. Stir in juice and herbs.
4 Serve lamb mixture with rice and lime wedges.

prep + cook time 30 minutes **serves** 4
nutritional count per serving 17.8g total fat (6.8g saturated fat); 2437kJ (583 cal); 67.5g carbohydrate; 35.4g protein; 4.1g fibre
tip If snake beans are unavailable, use green beans.

tonkatsu-don

3 cups (750ml) water

1½ cups (300g) sushi rice

4 pork steaks (600g)

¼ cup (35g) plain (all-purpose) flour

2 eggs

2 teaspoons water, extra

2 cups (100g) panko (japanese breadcrumbs)

1 tablespoon peanut oil

2 cloves garlic, sliced thinly

½ small wombok (napa cabbage) (350g), shredded finely

1 fresh small red thai (serrano) chilli, chopped finely

1 tablespoon mirin

1 tablespoon light soy sauce

vegetable oil, for deep-frying

2 green onions (scallions), sliced thinly

TONKATSU SAUCE

⅓ cup (80ml) tomato sauce

2 tablespoons japanese worcestershire sauce

2 tablespoons cooking sake

1 teaspoon japanese soy sauce

1 teaspoon japanese mustard

1 Make tonkatsu sauce.

2 Bring the water and rice to the boil in medium saucepan. Reduce heat; cook, covered tightly, over very low heat, about 15 minutes or until water is absorbed. Remove from heat; stand, covered, 10 minutes.

3 Meanwhile, pound pork gently with meat mallet; coat in flour, shake off excess. Dip pork in combined egg and extra water then coat in breadcrumbs.

4 Heat peanut oil in wok; cook garlic, stirring, until fragrant. Add wombok and chilli; cook, stirring, 1 minute. Transfer wombok mixture to large bowl with mirin and sauce; toss to combine. Cover to keep warm.

5 Heat vegetable oil in cleaned wok; deep-fry pork, in batches, turning occasionally, about 5 minutes or until golden brown. Drain on absorbent paper. Cut pork diagonally into 2cm (¾-inch) slices.

6 Divide rice among serving bowls; top with pork, wombok mixture then onion and drizzle with tonkatsu sauce.

tonkatsu sauce Bring ingredients to the boil in small saucepan. Remove from heat; cool.

prep + cook time 55 minutes **serves** 4
nutritional count per serving 31.6g total fat (8g saturated fat); 3595kJ (860 cal); 91g carbohydrate; 46.7g protein; 4g fibre
tips Panko breadcrumbs are available from most major supermarkets. If you can't find them, use stale breadcrumbs instead. We used sushi rice in this recipe, but you can also use arborio rice if it's more readily available. Prepared tonkatsu sauce is sold in most supermarkets and Asian food stores if you don't wish to make your own.

nasi goreng

720g (1½ pounds) cooked medium
king prawns (shrimp)

1 tablespoon peanut oil

175g (5½ ounces) dried chinese sausages,
sliced thickly

1 medium brown onion (150g), sliced thinly

1 medium red capsicum (bell peppers) (200g),
sliced thinly

2 fresh long red chillies, sliced thinly

2 cloves garlic, crushed

2cm (¾-inch) piece fresh ginger (10g), grated

1 teaspoon shrimp paste

4 cups (600g) cold cooked white long-grain rice

2 tablespoons kecap manis

1 tablespoon light soy sauce

4 green onions (scallions), sliced thinly

1 tablespoon peanut oil, extra

4 eggs

1 Shell and devein prawns, leaving tails intact.
2 Heat half the oil in wok; stir-fry sausage,
in batches, until browned. Remove from wok.
3 Heat remaining oil in wok; stir-fry onion,
capsicum, chilli, garlic, ginger and paste, until
vegetables soften. Add prawns and rice; stir-fry
2 minutes. Return sausage to wok with sauces
and half the green onion; stir-fry until combined.
4 Heat extra oil in large frying pan; fry eggs,
one side only, until just set.
5 Divide nasi goreng among serving plates,
top each with an egg; sprinkle with remaining
green onion.

prep + cook time 40 minutes **serves** 4
nutritional count per serving 25.7g total fat
(7.4g saturated fat); 2730kJ (653 cal);
48.5g carbohydrate; 54.7g protein; 3.3g fibre
tips Nasi goreng, which translates simply as
"fried rice" in Indonesia and Malaysia, was first
created to use up yesterday's leftovers.
You need to cook 2 cups (400g) white long-grain
rice the day before making this recipe. Spread it in
a thin layer on a tray and refrigerate it overnight.
Dried chinese sausages, also called lap cheong, are
usually made from pork and sold, strung together,
in supermarkets.

seafood laksa

12 uncooked medium king prawns (shrimp) (540g)

1 litre (4 cups) chicken stock

3¼ cups (810ml) coconut milk

4 kaffir lime leaves, shredded finely

155g (5 ounces) rice stick noodles

280g (9 ounces) scallops, roe removed

155g (5 ounces) marinated tofu, cut into 2cm (¾-inch) pieces

2 tablespoons lime juice

2 cups (160g) bean sprouts

4 green onions (scallions), sliced thinly

1 fresh long red chilli, sliced thinly

½ cup loosely packed fresh coriander (cilantro) leaves

LAKSA PASTE

3 dried medium chillies

⅓ cup (80ml) boiling water

2 teaspoons peanut oil

1 small brown onion (80g), chopped coarsely

2 cloves garlic, quartered

2cm (¾-inch) piece fresh ginger (10g), grated

10cm (4-inch) stick fresh lemon grass (20g), chopped finely

1 tablespoon halved, unroasted, unsalted macadamias

1 tablespoon coarsely chopped fresh coriander (cilantro) root and stem mixture

½ teaspoon each ground turmeric and ground coriander

¼ cup loosely packed fresh mint leaves

1 Make laksa paste.

2 Meanwhile, shell and devein prawns, leaving tails intact.

3 Cook paste in large saucepan, stirring, about 5 minutes or until fragrant. Stir in stock, coconut milk and lime leaves; bring to the boil. Reduce heat; simmer, covered, 20 minutes.

4 Meanwhile, place noodles in large heatproof bowl, cover with boiling water; stand until tender, drain.

5 Add prawns to laksa mixture; simmer, uncovered, about 5 minutes or until prawns change colour. Add scallops and tofu; simmer, uncovered, about 3 minutes or until scallops change colour. Remove from heat; stir in juice.

6 Divide noodles among serving bowls; ladle laksa into bowls, top with sprouts, onion, chilli and coriander leaves.

laksa paste Cover chillies with the water in small heatproof bowl, stand 10 minutes; drain. Blend or process chillies with remaining ingredients until mixture is smooth.

prep + cook time 1 hour 15 minutes **serves** 6
nutritional count per serving 35.4g total fat (25.9g saturated fat); 2207kJ (528 cal); 25.1g carbohydrate; 25.7g protein; 5g fibre

thai beef salad

¼ cup (60ml) fish sauce

¼ cup (60ml) lime juice

500g (1 pound) beef rump steak

3 lebanese cucumbers (390g),
sliced thinly lengthways

4 fresh small red thai (serrano) chillies,
sliced thinly

4 green onions (scallions), sliced thinly

250g (8 ounces) cherry tomatoes, halved

¼ cup firmly packed fresh vietnamese mint leaves

½ cup each firmly packed fresh coriander
(cilantro) leaves and fresh thai basil leaves

1 tablespoon grated palm sugar

2 teaspoons soy sauce

1 clove garlic, crushed

1 Combine 2 tablespoons of the fish sauce and
1 tablespoon of the juice in medium bowl with beef;
toss beef to coat in marinade. Cover; refrigerate
3 hours or overnight.

2 Drain beef; discard marinade. Cook beef on
heated oiled grill plate (or grill or grill pan)
until cooked as desired. Cover; stand 5 minutes.
Slice beef thinly.

3 Meanwhile, combine cucumber, chilli, onion,
tomato and herbs in large bowl.

4 Place sugar, soy sauce, garlic, remaining
fish sauce and remaining juice in screw-top jar;
shake well.

5 Add sliced beef to salad with dressing; toss
gently to combine.

prep + cook time 35 minutes (+ refrigeration)
serves 4
nutritional count per serving 8.7g total fat
(3.8g saturated fat); 986kJ (236 cal);
8.2g carbohydrate; 30.6g protein; 3.4g fibre
tips Thai basil is available from most supermarkets.
Use traditional basil instead if you cannot find any.
We used a vegetable peeler to slice the cucumbers
thinly into ribbons.

DESSERTS TO DIE FOR These after-dinner treats, laced with exotic flavours and spices, are surprisingly simple to make. Serve with french vanilla ice-cream, tart fruit or rich double cream for the most heavenly end to a delicious meal.

new york cheesecake

375g (12 ounces) plain sweet biscuits

185g (6 ounces) unsalted butter, melted

750g (1½ pounds) cream cheese, softened

2 teaspoons finely grated orange rind

1 teaspoon finely grated lemon rind

1 cup (220g) caster (superfine) sugar

3 eggs

¾ cup (180g) sour cream

¼ cup (60ml) lemon juice

SOUR CREAM TOPPING

1 cup (240g) sour cream

2 tablespoons caster (superfine) sugar

2 teaspoons lemon juice

1 Process biscuits until fine. Add butter, process until combined. Press mixture over base and side of 24cm (9½-inch) springform tin. Place tin on oven tray; refrigerate 30 minutes.

2 Preheat oven to 180°C/350°F.

3 Beat cream cheese, rinds and sugar in medium bowl with electric mixer until smooth. Beat in eggs, one at a time, then sour cream and juice. Pour filling into tin.

4 Bake cheesecake 1¼ hours. Remove from oven; cool 15 minutes.

5 Make sour cream topping; spread over filling. Bake cheesecake further 20 minutes; cool in oven with door ajar. Refrigerate 3 hours or overnight.

sour cream topping Combine ingredients in small bowl.

prep + cook time 2 hours 30 minutes
(+ refrigeration & cooling) **serves** 12
nutritional count per serving 53.4g total fat
(33.1g saturated fat); 2902kJ (693 cal);
46g carbohydrate; 9.9g protein; 0.6g fibre

rice pudding with cinnamon & vanilla bean

3 cups (750ml) milk

¼ cup (55g) caster (superfine) sugar

2 x 5cm (2-inch) strips lemon rind

1 vanilla bean, split lengthways

1 cinnamon stick

⅓ cup (65g) white medium-grain rice

3 egg yolks

⅓ cup (35g) roasted walnuts, chopped coarsely

¼ teaspoon ground cinnamon

1 Combine milk, sugar and rind in medium saucepan; bring to the boil, stirring occasionally. Add vanilla bean and cinnamon stick, gradually stir in rice; cook, covered tightly, over low heat, stirring occasionally, about 40 minutes or until rice is tender. Remove from heat. Discard rind, cinnamon stick and vanilla bean; quickly stir in egg yolks.

2 Serve pudding sprinkled with nuts and ground cinnamon.

prep + cook time 55 minutes **serves** 4
nutritional count per serving 11.6g total fat (5.6g saturated fat); 1282kJ (306 cal); 42g carbohydrate; 9.8g protein; 0.4g fibre
tip This dish can be served warm or at room temperature.

soft-centred chocolate cakes

155g (5 ounces) dark eating (semi-sweet) chocolate, chopped coarsely

125g (4 ounces) unsalted butter, chopped

3 teaspoons instant coffee granules

2 eggs

2 egg yolks

⅓ cup (75g) caster (superfine) sugar

¼ cup (35g) plain (all-purpose) flour

2 teaspoons cocoa powder

1 Preheat oven to 200°C/400°F. Grease six-hole (¾-cup/180ml) texas muffin pan well with softened butter.

2 Stir chocolate, butter and coffee in small saucepan, over low heat, until smooth; cool 10 minutes. Transfer mixture to large bowl.

3 Beat eggs, egg yolks and sugar in small bowl with electric mixer until thick and creamy. Fold egg mixture and sifted flour into barely warm chocolate mixture.

4 Spoon mixture into pan holes; bake 12 minutes.

5 Gently turn puddings onto serving plates, top-side down. Dust with sifted cocoa powder and serve immediately.

prep + cook time 40 minutes **makes** 6
nutritional count per cake 28.5g total fat (16.9g saturated fat); 1686kJ (403 cal); 33.3g carbohydrate; 5.5g protein; 0.7g fibre
tip These cakes should be served shortly after they come out of the oven. If they are allowed to sit for a few minutes, the gooey centre will firm up and the chocolate won't ooze out when they're cut.
warning The melted chocolate centre will be hot, so take care when biting into the cakes.
serving suggestion Serve with fresh raspberries and softly whipped cream.

clove panna cotta with fresh figs

1 teaspoon whole cloves

1¼ cups (310ml) thickened (heavy) cream

⅔ cup (160ml) milk

2 teaspoons gelatine

2 tablespoons caster (superfine) sugar

½ teaspoon vanilla extract

2 tablespoons honey

4 medium fresh figs (240g), quartered

1 Grease four ½-cup (125ml) moulds.

2 Place cloves, cream and milk in small saucepan; stand 10 minutes. Sprinkle gelatine and sugar over cream mixture; stir over low heat, without boiling, until gelatine and sugar dissolve. Stir in extract. Strain into medium jug; cool to room temperature.

3 Pour cream mixture into moulds. Cover; refrigerate 3 hours or until set.

4 Stir honey in small saucepan until warm.

5 Turn panna cotta onto serving plates; serve with figs drizzled with warm honey.

prep + cook time 30 minutes (+ cooling & refrigeration) **serves** 4
nutritional count per serving 29.3g total fat (19.2g saturated fat); 1639kJ (392 cal); 29.1g carbohydrate; 5.1g protein; 1.3g fibre
tip It is fine to use just one 300ml carton of cream for this recipe.

tiramisu

2 tablespoons ground espresso coffee

1 cup (250ml) boiling water

½ cup (125ml) marsala

250g (8 ounces) sponge finger biscuits

1¼ cups (310ml) thickened (heavy) cream

¼ cup (40g) icing (confectioners') sugar

500g (1 pound) mascarpone cheese

2 tablespoons marsala, extra

2 teaspoons cocoa powder

1 Combine coffee and the water in coffee plunger; stand 2 minutes before plunging. Combine coffee mixture and marsala in medium heatproof bowl; cool 10 minutes.

2 Place half the biscuits, in single layer, over base of deep 2-litre (8-cup) dish; drizzle with half the coffee mixture.

3 Beat cream and sifted icing sugar in small bowl until soft peaks form; transfer to large bowl. Fold in combined mascarpone cheese and extra marsala.

4 Spread half the cream mixture over biscuits in dish. Submerge remaining biscuits, one at a time, in remaining coffee mixture, taking care the biscuits do not become so soggy that they fall apart; place over cream layer. Top biscuit layer with remaining cream mixture. Cover; refrigerate 3 hours or overnight.

5 Serve tiramisu dusted with sifted cocoa.

prep time 30 minutes (+ refrigeration) **serves** 8
nutritional count per serving 45g total fat (29.9g saturated fat); 2391kJ (572 cal); 25.8g carbohydrate; 6.5g protein; 0.5g fibre
tips It is fine to use just one 300ml carton of cream for this recipe.
People are often confused about whether to regard mascarpone as a cheese or a thick cream. It is, in fact, a fresh triple-cream cheese originating in Italy's Lombardy region, and probably first became known to us when tiramisu was the dessert du jour in the mid-1980s. Like most wonderful things, there is no real substitute for mascarpone, but some recipes can be adapted to use soft cream cheese, sour cream or ricotta – or a combination of all three.

ginger sticky date pudding

1 cup (140g) seeded dried dates

¼ cup (55g) glacé ginger

1 teaspoon bicarbonate of soda

1 cup (250ml) boiling water

50g (1½ ounces) unsalted butter, chopped

½ cup (110g) firmly packed light brown sugar

2 eggs

1 cup (150g) self-raising flour

1 teaspoon ground ginger

BUTTERSCOTCH SAUCE

1¼ cups (310ml) pouring cream

¾ cup (165g) firmly packed light brown sugar

75g (2½ ounces) unsalted butter, chopped

1 Preheat oven to 200°C/400°F. Grease deep 20cm (8-inch) round cake pan; line base with baking paper.
2 Combine dates, ginger, soda and the water in food processor; stand 5 minutes then add butter and sugar. Process until mixture is almost smooth. Add eggs, flour and ginger; process until combined. Pour mixture into pan.
3 Bake pudding about 45 minutes. Stand in pan 10 minutes before turning onto serving plate.
4 Meanwhile, make butterscotch sauce.
5 Serve pudding warm with sauce.
butterscotch sauce Stir ingredients in medium saucepan over low heat until sauce is smooth.

prep + cook time 55 minutes **serves** 8
nutritional count per serving 30.1g total fat (19.6g saturated fat); 2337kJ (559 cal); 65.1g carbohydrate; 4.7g protein; 2.4g fibre
tip It is fine to use just one 300ml carton of cream for this recipe.
serving suggestion Serve with vanilla ice-cream.

COUNTRY

Generous hospitality and a home-cooked meal are a
traditional country greeting. Regional towns are now
popping up as sophisticated food centres brimming
with fresh produce and artisan products.

7.

BIG BREAKFAST Chances are you've had an early morning. You might have even been out in the paddocks already. Come inside to the warmth of the kitchen and enjoy a wholesome country breakfast, in readiness for a big day ahead.

cooked english breakfast

50g (1½ ounces) butter

300g (9½ ounces) button mushrooms, halved

1 tablespoon fresh thyme leaves

8 chipolata sausages (240g)

4 rindless bacon slices (260g)

2 medium tomatoes (300g), halved

1 tablespoon vegetable oil

8 eggs

1 Heat butter in medium saucepan; cook mushrooms, stirring, about 5 minutes or until tender. Sprinkle with thyme, season to taste; cover to keep warm.

2 Cook sausages and bacon in heated oiled large frying pan. Remove from pan; cover to keep warm. Drain fat from pan.

3 Preheat grill (broiler).

4 Place tomato, cut-side up, on oven tray; grill tomato until browned lightly.

5 Meanwhile, heat oil in same large frying pan; cook eggs until done to your liking.

6 Serve mushrooms, sausages, bacon, tomato and eggs with toast, if you like.

prep + cook time 20 minutes **serves** 4
nutritional count per serving 47.7g total fat (20.2g saturated fat); 2424kJ (580 cal); 3.5g carbohydrate; 34.6g protein; 2.4g fibre

scrambled eggs

scrambled eggs

250g (8 ounces) cherry tomatoes

1 tablespoon olive oil

8 thin rindless bacon slices (240g)

8 eggs

½ cup (125ml) pouring cream

2 tablespoons finely chopped fresh chives

30g (1 ounce) butter

4 slices crusty white bread (280g), toasted

1 Preheat grill (broiler).
2 Toss tomatoes in oil; place on oven tray with bacon. Cook bacon and tomato under grill until bacon is crisp and tomato skins start to split. Cover to keep warm.
3 Meanwhile, lightly beat eggs, cream and half the chives in medium bowl with a fork.
4 Heat butter in large frying pan over medium heat. Add egg mixture, wait a few seconds, then use a wide spatula to gently scrape the set egg mixture along the base of the pan; cook until creamy and just set.
5 Serve toast topped with egg, bacon and tomatoes; sprinkle with remaining chives.

prep + cook time 25 minutes **serves** 4
nutritional count per serving 52g total fat
(23.9g saturated fat); 3223kJ (771 cal);
40g carbohydrate; 37.6g protein; 2.5g fibre

smoky beans with chorizo

1 large red onion (300g), chopped coarsely

1 cured chorizo sausage (170g), chopped coarsely

1 large red capsicum (bell pepper) (350g), chopped coarsely

2 teaspoons smoked paprika

800g (1½ pounds) canned borlotti beans, rinsed, drained

800g (1½ pounds) canned crushed tomatoes

2 tablespoons coarsely chopped fresh flat-leaf parsley

1 Heat oiled large saucepan; cook onion, chorizo and capsicum, stirring, until vegetables are tender. Add paprika; cook, stirring, until fragrant.
2 Add beans and undrained tomatoes to pan; bring to the boil. Reduce heat; simmer, uncovered, about 5 minutes or until sauce is thickened. Season to taste. Serve sprinkled with parsley.

prep + cook time 10 minutes **serves** 6
nutritional count per serving 9.4g total fat
(3.3g saturated fat); 1225kJ (293 cal);
33g carbohydrate; 15.9g protein; 6.2g fibre
serving suggestion Serve with crusty bread.

{photograph page 142}

smoky beans with chorizo {recipe page 141}

tomato & egg muffin {recipe page 144}

tomato & egg muffin

cooking-oil spray

2 eggs

2 multigrain english muffins (130g), split

1 small tomato (90g), sliced thinly

2 teaspoons balsamic vinegar

1 Spray medium frying pan with cooking oil. Fry eggs until cooked as you like.
2 Meanwhile, toast muffins.
3 Divide tomato between two muffin halves; sprinkle with vinegar, top with eggs, then remaining muffin halves.

prep + cook time 10 minutes **makes** 2
nutritional count per muffin 7.3g total fat (1.9g saturated fat); 953kJ (228 cal); 24.2g carbohydrate; 14.5g protein; 3.9g fibre
tip You could poach the eggs instead, if you like.

{photograph page 143}

bircher muesli

2 cups (180g) rolled oats

1¼ cups (310ml) apple juice

1 cup (280g) yogurt

2 medium green-skinned apples (300g)

¼ cup (35g) roasted slivered almonds

¼ cup (40g) currants

¼ cup (20g) toasted shredded coconut

1 teaspoon ground cinnamon

½ cup (140g) yogurt, extra

2 tablespoons honey

1 Combine oats, juice and yogurt in medium bowl. Cover; refrigerate overnight.
2 Peel, core and coarsely grate one apple; stir into oat mixture with nuts, currants, coconut and cinnamon.
3 Core and thinly slice remaining apple. Serve muesli topped with extra yogurt and apple slices; drizzle with honey.

prep time 20 minutes (+ refrigeration) **serves** 6
nutritional count per serving 10.4g total fat (4.1g saturated fat); 1187kJ (284 cal); 37g carbohydrate; 8.2g protein; 4.3g fibre

bircher muesli

raspberry hotcakes with honeycomb butter

2 cups (500ml) buttermilk

2 eggs

40g (1½ ounces) butter, melted

2 teaspoons vanilla extract

2 cups (300g) self-raising flour

⅓ cup (75g) caster (superfine) sugar

pinch salt

150g (4½ ounces) frozen raspberries, thawed

HONEYCOMB BUTTER

125g (4 ounces) unsalted butter, softened

⅓ cup (12g) finely chopped honeycomb

1 Make honeycomb butter.

2 Whisk buttermilk, eggs, butter and vanilla in medium jug until combined. Sift flour, sugar and salt into medium bowl; gradually whisk in buttermilk mixture until smooth.

3 Cook hotcakes, in batches, by dropping ¼ cup batter for each hotcake into heated oiled large frying pan; sprinkle each hotcake with six raspberries. Cook hotcakes until bubbles appear on the surface; turn, brown other side. Remove from pan; cover to keep warm. Repeat with remaining batter to make 12 hotcakes.

4 Serve hotcakes with honeycomb butter.

honeycomb butter Beat butter in small bowl with electric mixer until light and fluffy; stir in honeycomb. Set aside at room temperature.

prep + cook time 40 minutes **serves** 4
nutritional count per serving 40.1g total fat (24.9g saturated fat); 2922kJ (699 cal); 84g carbohydrate; 16.8g protein; 4.9g fibre
tips Transfer the cooked hotcakes to an oven tray or heatproof plate, cover with foil and place in a preheated 120°C/250°F oven to keep them warm while you cook the remaining hotcakes.
Plain, uncoated honeycomb is available from speciality food stores, health food stores, good delicatessens and confectionery shops.
serving suggestion Serve with maple syrup and extra raspberries.

MORNING TEA Baking in the country is seen as an art, so morning tea, with its scones, cakes and slices, is always something to look forward to. Sweet things are made to share – cut and serve with a cup of tea.

vanilla slice

2 sheets puff pastry

½ cup (110g) caster (superfine) sugar

½ cup (75g) cornflour (cornstarch)

¼ cup (30g) custard powder

2½ cups (625ml) milk

30g (1 ounce) unsalted butter

1 egg yolk

1 teaspoon vanilla extract

¾ cup (180ml) thickened (heavy) cream

PASSIONFRUIT ICING

1½ cups (240g) icing (confectioners') sugar

1 teaspoon softened butter

¼ cup (60ml) passionfruit pulp

1 Preheat oven to 240°C/475°F. Grease deep 22cm (9-inch) square cake pan; line with foil, extending foil 10cm (4 inches) over sides of pan.
2 Place each pastry sheet on separate greased oven tray. Bake about 15 minutes; cool. Flatten pastry with hand; place one pastry sheet in pan, trim to fit if necessary.
3 Meanwhile, combine sugar, cornflour and custard powder in medium saucepan; gradually add milk, stirring until smooth. Add butter; stir over heat until mixture boils and thickens. Simmer, stirring, 3 minutes or until thick and smooth. Remove from heat; stir in egg yolk and extract. Cover surface of custard with plastic wrap; cool to room temperature.

4 Make passionfruit icing.
5 Beat cream in small bowl with electric mixer until firm peaks form. Fold cream into custard, in two batches.
6 Spread custard mixture over pastry in pan. Top with remaining pastry, trim to fit if necessary; press down slightly. Spread icing over pastry.
7 Refrigerate slice 3 hours or overnight.
passionfruit icing Place sifted icing sugar, butter and passionfruit pulp in small heatproof bowl over small saucepan of simmering water; stir until icing is spreadable.

prep + cook time 55 minutes (+ cooling & refrigeration) **makes** 16
nutritional count per piece 12.6g total fat (7.6g saturated fat); 1158kJ (237 cal); 37.2g carbohydrate; 3.1g protein; 0.8g fibre
tip It's best to store any leftover slice in large pieces, so if you think it won't all be eaten or you want to save some for later, keep a portion without cutting it into squares or bars. Keep the piece of slice as airtight as possible in a resealable plastic bag or an airtight container, and cut it just before you're ready to serve.

date & walnut loaf

60g (2 ounces) unsalted butter

1 cup (250ml) boiling water

1 cup (180g) finely chopped dried dates

½ teaspoon bicarbonate of soda (baking soda)

1 cup (220g) firmly packed light brown sugar

2 cups (300g) self-raising flour

½ cup (60g) coarsely chopped walnuts

1 egg, beaten lightly

1 Preheat oven to 180°C/350°F. Grease two 8cm x 19cm (3¼-inch x 7½-inch) nut roll tins; line bases with baking paper. Place tins upright on oven tray.
2 Stir butter and the water in medium saucepan over low heat until butter melts. Remove from heat; stir in dates and soda, then remaining ingredients. Spoon mixture into tins; replace lids.
3 Bake rolls about 50 minutes. Stand rolls in tins 5 minutes; remove ends (top and bottom), shake tins gently to release rolls onto wire rack to cool. Serve rolls sliced with butter.

prep + cook time 1 hour 10 minutes **serves** 20
nutritional count per serving 5g total fat
(1.9g saturated fat); 702kJ (168 cal);
27.4g carbohydrate; 2.5g protein; 1.6g fibre

tips If you can't find nut roll tins, you can make your own from tall 850ml (8cm x 17cm/3¼-inch x 6½-inch) fruit juice cans. You'll need to remove one end from each can by using a can opener that cuts just below the rim. Wash and dry cans thoroughly before greasing.
It is important that you do not fill nut roll tins with too much mixture. The nut rolls rise surprisingly high; both because the tin is narrow and because the cooking method approximates that of steaming. As a rough guide, the tins should be filled just a little over halfway.
Some nut roll tins open along the side; be certain these are closed properly before baking. Some also have lids with tiny holes in them to allow steam to escape; make sure these are not used on the bottom of the tins.

Callicoma Hill, New South Wales

neenish tarts

1¾ cups (260g) plain (all-purpose) flour

¼ cup (40g) icing (confectioners') sugar

185g (6 ounces) cold unsalted butter, chopped coarsely

1 egg yolk

2 teaspoons iced water, approximately

⅓ cup (110g) strawberry jam

MOCK CREAM

¾ cup (165g) caster (superfine) sugar

⅓ cup (80ml) water

1½ tablespoons milk

½ teaspoon gelatine

185g (6 ounces) unsalted butter, softened

1 teaspoon vanilla extract

GLACE ICING

1½ cups (240g) icing (confectioners') sugar

15g (½ ounce) unsalted butter, melted

2 tablespoons hot milk, approximately

pink food colouring

1 teaspoon cocoa powder

1 Process flour, sugar and butter until crumbly. With motor operating, add egg yolk and enough of the water to make ingredients come together. Turn dough onto floured surface, knead gently until smooth. Wrap pastry in plastic; refrigerate 30 minutes.

2 Grease two 12-hole (2-tablespoon/40ml) deep flat-based patty pans. Roll out half the pastry between sheets of baking paper until 3mm (⅛-inch) thick. Cut out 12 x 7.5cm (3-inch) rounds; press rounds into holes of one pan. Prick bases of cases well with a fork. Repeat with remaining pastry. Refrigerate 30 minutes.

3 Preheat oven to 220°C/425°F.

4 Bake cases about 12 minutes. Stand cases in pans 5 minutes before transferring to wire rack to cool.

5 Meanwhile, make mock cream, then glacé icing.

6 Spoon jam into cases; fill cases with mock cream, level tops with spatula. Spread pink icing over half of each tart; spread chocolate icing over other half.

mock cream Stir sugar, ¼ cup of the water and milk in small saucepan over low heat, without boiling, until sugar dissolves. Sprinkle gelatine over remaining water in small jug; stir into milk mixture until gelatine dissolves. Cool to room temperature. Beat butter and extract in small bowl with electric mixer until as white as possible. With motor operating, gradually beat in cold milk mixture; beat until light and fluffy.

glacé icing Sift icing sugar into medium bowl; stir in butter and enough of the milk to make a thick paste. Divide icing between two small heatproof bowls; tint icing in one bowl with pink colouring and the other with sifted cocoa. Stir each bowl over small saucepan of simmering water until icing is spreadable.

prep + cook time 1 hour 45 minutes (+ refrigeration & cooling) **makes** 24
nutritional count per tart 13.6g total fat (8.8g saturated); 1016kJ (243 cal); 29.7g carbohydrate; 1.6g protein; 0.5g fibre

carrot cake with lemon cream cheese frosting

3 eggs

1⅓ cups (295g) firmly packed light brown sugar

1 cup (250ml) vegetable oil

3 cups firmly packed, coarsely grated carrot

1 cup (110g) coarsely chopped walnuts

2½ cups (375g) self-raising flour

½ teaspoon bicarbonate of soda (baking soda)

2 teaspoons mixed spice

LEMON CREAM CHEESE FROSTING

30g (1 ounce) unsalted butter, softened

80g (2½ ounces) cream cheese, softened

1 teaspoon finely grated lemon rind

1½ cups (240g) icing (confectioners') sugar

1 Preheat oven to 180°C/350°F. Grease deep 22cm (9-inch) round cake pan; line base with baking paper.

2 Beat eggs, sugar and oil in small bowl with electric mixer until thick and creamy. Transfer mixture to large bowl; stir in carrot and nuts then sifted dry ingredients. Pour mixture into pan.

3 Bake cake about 1¼ hours. Stand cake in pan 5 minutes before turning, top-side up, onto wire rack to cool.

4 Meanwhile, make lemon cream cheese frosting.

5 Spread cake with frosting.

lemon cream cheese frosting Beat butter, cream cheese and rind in small bowl with electric mixer until light and fluffy; gradually beat in sifted icing sugar.

prep + cook time 1 hour 45 minutes **serves** 12
nutritional count per serving 31.4g total fat (6g saturated fat); 2404kJ (575 cal); 67.7g carbohydrate; 6.9g protein; 2.9g fibre
tips You need three large carrots (540g) for this recipe. Cake will keep in an airtight container, in the fridge, for up to four days.

anzac biscuits
{recipe page 160}

Callicoma Hill, New South Wales

anzac biscuits

125g (4 ounces) butter, chopped

2 tablespoons golden syrup or treacle

1 tablespoon water

½ teaspoon bicarbonate of soda (baking soda)

1 cup (220g) firmly packed light brown sugar

½ cup (40g) desiccated coconut

1 cup (90g) rolled oats

1 cup (150g) plain (all-purpose) flour

1 Preheat oven to 160°C/325°F. Line oven trays with baking paper.
2 Stir butter, syrup and the water in large saucepan over low heat until smooth. Remove from heat; stir in soda, then remaining ingredients.
3 Roll tablespoons of mixture into balls; place about 5cm (2 inches) apart on trays, flatten slightly.
4 Bake biscuits about 20 minutes; cool on trays.

prep + cook time 35 minutes **makes** 25
nutritional count per biscuit 5.4g total fat (3.5g saturated fat); 492kJ (118 cal); 16.7g carbohydrate; 1.2g protein; 0.8g fibre
tips Anzac biscuits should still feel soft when they're cooked; they will firm up as they cool. Store the biscuits in an airtight container at room temperature for up to a week.

{photograph page 158}

jam roll

3 eggs, separated

½ cup (110g) caster (superfine) sugar

2 tablespoons hot milk

¾ cup (110g) self-raising flour

¼ cup (55g) caster (superfine) sugar, extra

½ cup (160g) jam, warmed

1 Preheat oven to 200°C/400°F. Grease 25cm x 30cm (10-inch x 12-inch) swiss roll pan; line base with baking paper, extending paper 5cm (2 inches) over short sides.
2 Beat egg whites in small bowl with electric mixer until soft peaks form; add sugar, 1 tablespoon at a time, beating until dissolved between additions. With motor operating, add egg yolks, one at a time, beating until mixture is pale and thick; this will take about 10 minutes.
3 Pour hot milk down side of bowl; add triple-sifted flour. Working quickly, use plastic spatula to fold milk and flour through egg mixture. Pour mixture into pan, gently spreading evenly into corners.
4 Bake cake about 8 minutes.
5 Meanwhile, place a piece of baking paper cut the same size as pan on board or bench; sprinkle evenly with extra sugar.
6 Turn cake immediately onto sugared paper; peel away lining paper. Use serrated knife to trim crisp edges from all sides of cake.
7 Using paper as a guide, gently roll warm cake loosely from one of the short sides. Unroll; spread evenly with jam. Reroll cake from same short side. Cool before serving.

prep + cook time 30 minutes **serves** 10
nutritional count per serving 1.9g total fat (0.6g saturated fat); 819kJ (196 cal); 40.5g carbohydrate; 3.3g protein; 0.6g fibre

jam roll

buttermilk scones with jam & cream

2½ cups (375g) self-raising flour

1 tablespoon caster (superfine) sugar

30g (1 ounce) unsalted butter, chopped

1¼ cups (310ml) buttermilk

¾ cup (240g) black cherry jam

1 cup (250ml) thick (double) cream

1 Preheat oven to 220°C/425°F. Grease 22cm (9-inch) square cake pan.

2 Sift flour and sugar into large bowl; rub in butter.

3 Add buttermilk. Use a knife to cut the buttermilk through the flour mixture to make a soft, sticky dough. Turn dough onto floured surface, knead gently until smooth.

4 Press dough out to 2cm (¾-inch) thickness, cut out 4cm (1½-inch) rounds. Place scones, just touching, in pan. Gently knead scraps of dough together; repeat process. Brush scones with a little extra buttermilk.

5 Bake scones about 15 minutes. Serve warm scones with jam and cream.

prep + cook time 35 minutes **makes** 25
nutritional count per scone 6.4g total fat (4.1g saturated fat); 583kJ (139 cal); 18.4g carbohydrate; 2.2g protein; 0.7g fibre
tips Scones are best made on the day of serving. They can be frozen for up to 3 months. Thaw in oven, wrapped in foil. You could substitute the thick cream for clotted cream or whipped thickened cream.

lamingtons

6 eggs

⅔ cup (150g) caster (superfine) sugar

⅓ cup (50g) cornflour (cornstarch)

½ cup (75g) plain (all-purpose) flour

⅓ cup (50g) self-raising flour

2 cups (160g) desiccated coconut

CHOCOLATE ICING

4 cups (640g) icing (confectioners') sugar

½ cup (50g) cocoa powder

15g (½ ounce) unsalted butter, melted

1 cup (250ml) milk

1 Preheat oven to 180°C/350°F. Grease 20cm x 30cm (8-inch x 12-inch) rectangular pan; line base and long sides with baking paper, extending paper 5cm (2 inches) over sides.

2 Beat eggs in large bowl with electric mixer about 10 minutes or until thick and creamy; gradually add sugar, beating until dissolved between additions. Triple-sift flours; fold into egg mixture. Spread mixture into pan.

3 Bake cake about 35 minutes. Turn immediately onto baking-paper-covered wire rack to cool.

4 Meanwhile, make chocolate icing.

5 Place coconut in medium bowl. Cut cake into 16 pieces. Dip each piece in icing; drain off excess, then toss squares in coconut. Place lamingtons on wire rack to set.

chocolate icing Sift icing sugar and cocoa in medium heatproof bowl; stir in butter and milk. Set bowl over medium saucepan of simmering water; stir until icing is of a coating consistency.

prep + cook time 50 minutes **makes** 16
nutritional count per lamington 10.4g total fat (7g saturated fat); 1438kJ (344 cal); 59.7g carbohydrate; 5.1g protein; 2g fibre

classic chocolate caramel slice

1 cup (150g) plain (all-purpose) flour

½ cup (110g) firmly packed light brown sugar

½ cup (40g) desiccated coconut

125g (4 ounces) unsalted butter, melted

60g (2 ounces) unsalted butter, extra

395g (12½ ounces) canned sweetened condensed milk

2 tablespoons golden syrup or treacle

185g (6 ounces) dark eating (semi-sweet) chocolate, chopped coarsely

2 teaspoons vegetable oil

1 Preheat oven to 180°C/350°F. Grease 20cm x 30cm (8-inch x 12-inch) rectangular pan; line base and long sides with baking paper, extending paper 5cm (2 inches) over sides.
2 Combine sifted flour, sugar and coconut in medium bowl; stir in butter. Press flour mixture firmly into pan; bake about 15 minutes. Cool.
3 Combine extra butter, condensed milk and syrup in medium saucepan; stir over low heat until smooth. Pour mixture over base. Bake about 15 minutes or until golden brown. Cool.
4 Stir chocolate and oil in medium heatproof bowl over medium saucepan of simmering water until smooth. Spread chocolate mixture over slice. Refrigerate about 30 minutes or until set before cutting slice using a hot knife.

prep + cook time 55 minutes (+ refrigeration)
makes 48
nutritional count per piece 5.8g total fat (3.7g saturated fat); 439kJ (105 cal); 12.4g carbohydrate; 1.3g protein; 0.3g fibre
tip Store slice in an airtight container for up to a week.

PUB FOOD Modern pub food is rustic, humble and uncomplicated. The focus is on a few key ingredients, and the trick is to cook them well. When making these classic dishes at home, start with good-quality produce and you won't go wrong.

lamb shank pies
with crushed peas & fetta

6 french-trimmed lamb shanks (1.5kg)

¼ cup (35g) plain (all-purpose) flour

1 tablespoon olive oil

2 medium brown onions (300g), chopped coarsely

2 medium carrots (240g), chopped coarsely

3 cloves garlic, crushed

½ teaspoon dried oregano

3 cups (750ml) salt-reduced chicken stock

1 cup (260g) bottled tomato pasta sauce

2 medium potatoes (400g), chopped coarsely

2 tablespoons lemon juice

2 tablespoons chopped fresh dill

2 sheets butter puff pastry

1 egg, beaten lightly

CRUSHED PEAS & FETTA

2½ cups (300g) frozen baby peas

1 tablespoon torn fresh mint leaves

1 tablespoon olive oil

⅓ cup (65g) crumbled fetta cheese

1 Preheat oven to 180°C/350°F.
2 Toss shanks in flour; shake away excess. Heat oil in medium flameproof dish; cook shanks until browned. Remove from dish.
3 Add onion and carrot to same dish; cook, stirring, until soft. Add garlic and oregano; cook, stirring, until fragrant. Add stock and sauce; bring to the boil. Return shanks to dish; cover tightly. Transfer to oven; cook for 1½ hours.
4 Add potato to dish; cover, cook 30 minutes or until lamb and potato are tender. If sauce is too thin, simmer, uncovered, over medium heat until thickened slightly. Stir in juice and dill; season to taste. Cool 10 minutes.
5 Remove half the meat from the shanks; cut meat into smaller pieces. Refrigerate lamb mixture and shanks 3 hours or until cold. Remove fat from surface of dish.
6 Preheat oven to 220°C/425°F.
7 Divide lamb mixture and shanks among six 2-cup (500ml) deep ovenproof dishes, standing shanks upright in dishes. Cut out pastry slightly larger than the tops of the dishes. Cut a small cross in the centre of each pastry. Place pastry over pies, inserting shank bone through cross in pastry. Brush pastry with egg. Place dishes on oven tray.
8 Bake pies about 20 minutes or until browned.
9 Meanwhile, make crushed peas & fetta.
10 Serve pies with crushed peas & fetta.
crushed peas & fetta Boil, steam or microwave peas until tender; drain. Crush peas lightly with fork. Stir in mint and oil; season to taste. Gently stir in cheese.

prep + cook time 3 hours 10 minutes
(+ cooling & refrigeration) **serves** 6
nutritional count per serving 36g total fat
(15.5g saturated fat); 2876kJ (688 cal);
45.3g carbohydrate; 42.1g protein; 7.6g fibre

beef shiraz pies

750g (1½ pounds) beef chuck steak, chopped coarsely

2 tablespoons plain (all-purpose) flour

¼ cup (60ml) olive oil

1 medium brown onion (150g), chopped finely

1 medium carrot (120g), chopped finely

2 sticks celery (300g), trimmed, chopped finely

2 cloves garlic, crushed

½ cup (125ml) dry red wine

½ cup (125ml) beef stock

410g (13 ounces) canned diced tomatoes

2 tablespoons fresh thyme leaves

1 egg, beaten lightly

SOUR CREAM PASTRY

2¼ cups (335g) plain (all-purpose) flour

125g (4 ounces) cold butter, chopped coarsely

½ cup (120g) sour cream

1 Preheat oven to 180°C/350°F. Oil six-hole (¾-cup/180ml) texas muffin pan.

2 Toss beef in flour, shake away excess. Heat half the oil in large frying pan; cook beef, in batches, until browned. Transfer beef to 3-litre (12-cup) ovenproof dish.

3 Heat remaining oil in same pan; cook onion, carrot, celery and garlic, stirring, until softened. Add wine; bring to the boil. Stir in stock, undrained tomatoes and thyme; bring to the boil. Pour over beef. Cook, covered, 2 hours. Season to taste; cool.

4 Meanwhile, make sour cream pastry.

5 Roll two-thirds of the pastry between sheets of baking paper until large enough to cut six 13cm (5¼-inch) rounds; press pastry into pan holes. Brush edges with egg. Divide beef mixture among pastry cases.

6 Cut six 9cm (3½-inch) rounds from remaining pastry; place pastry over filling. Press edges firmly to seal; brush tops with egg. Cut a small slit in top of each pie.

7 Bake pies about 30 minutes or until browned. Stand pies 5 minutes before serving.

sour cream pastry Process flour and butter until crumbly. Add sour cream; process until ingredients barely cling together. Knead dough on floured surface until smooth. Wrap pastry in plastic; refrigerate 30 minutes.

prep + cook time 3 hours (+ cooling & refrigeration)
makes 6
nutritional count per pie 45.7g total fat (21.6g saturated fat); 3202kJ (766 cal); 46.5g carbohydrate; 37.1g protein; 4.4g fibre
tips Sour cream pastry is lighter in texture but richer in flavour than basic shortcrust pastry. It is extremely easy to handle and may be used for both savoury and sweet pies. We used shiraz for this recipe, but you can use any red wine you like.

Berry, New South Wales

oung, New South Wales

lamb burgers with
yogurt dressing & beetroot relish

500g (1 pound) minced (ground) lamb

1 small brown onion (80g), chopped finely

2 cloves garlic, crushed

1 teaspoon ground cumin

1 egg, beaten lightly

1 tablespoon olive oil

1 loaf turkish bread (430g)

50g (1½ ounces) baby rocket (arugula) leaves

BEETROOT RELISH

4 medium beetroot (700g), grated coarsely

1 small brown onion (80g), chopped finely

⅓ cup (80ml) water

½ cup (110g) white (granulated) sugar

⅔ cup (160ml) cider vinegar

YOGURT DRESSING

¾ cup (200g) Greek-style yogurt

1 tablespoon finely chopped fresh mint

½ teaspoon ground cumin

1 Make beetroot relish.
2 Meanwhile, combine lamb, onion, garlic, cumin and egg in medium bowl; season. Shape mixture into four patties.
3 Cook patties on heated oiled grill pan (or grill or barbecue). Remove from barbecue; cover to keep warm.
4 Make yogurt dressing.
5 Cut bread into quarters; halve quarters horizontally. Toast bread on heated oiled barbecue, until browned both sides.
6 Place rocket, patties, yogurt dressing and relish between bread.

beetroot relish Cook beetroot, onion and the water in large frying pan, covered, 15 minutes or until beetroot is tender. Stir in sugar and vinegar; cook, covered, stirring occasionally, 20 minutes. Uncover; cook, stirring occasionally, 10 minutes or until liquid evaporates.

yogurt dressing Combine ingredients in small bowl.

prep + cook time 1 hour 15 minutes **makes** 4
nutritional count per burger 22g total fat
(7.9g saturated fat); 3173kJ (759 cal);
95.9g carbohydrate; 43.6g protein; 8.6g fibre

red wine & garlic beef ribs

2.5kg (5 pounds) slabs barbecue beef ribs

½ cup (125ml) dry red wine

¼ cup (60ml) worcestershire sauce

2 tablespoons wholegrain mustard

⅓ cup (95g) tomato paste

¼ cup (55g) firmly packed light brown sugar

3 cloves garlic, crushed

1 tablespoon fresh thyme leaves

OLIVE & BASIL MASH

750g (1½ pounds) potatoes, chopped coarsely

40g (1½ ounces) butter

½ cup (125ml) pouring cream, heated

¼ cup (40g) finely chopped seeded black olives

1 tablespoon finely chopped fresh basil

1 Combine ribs with remaining ingredients in large non-metallic baking dish; season. Cover; refrigerate 3 hours or overnight.

2 Drain ribs; reserve marinade. Cook ribs on heated oiled covered grill pan (or grill or barbecue), turning occasionally, about 1 hour. Remove ribs from barbecue; cover, stand 5 minutes.

3 Meanwhile, make olive & basil mash.

4 Bring reserved marinade to the boil in small saucepan; boil, uncovered, about 3 minutes or until sauce is thickened slightly.

5 Cut ribs into pieces; serve with mash and sauce.

olive & basil mash Boil, steam or microwave potatoes until tender; drain. Mash potatoes with butter and cream until smooth. Stir in olives and basil; season to taste.

prep + cook time 1 hour 20 minutes (+ refrigeration)
serves 4
nutritional count per serving 40.1g total fat (22g saturated fat); 3411kJ (816 cal); 43.8g carbohydrate; 63.5g protein; 4.4g fibre

moussaka

¼ cup (60ml) olive oil

2 large eggplants (1kg), sliced thinly

1 large brown onion (200g), chopped finely

2 cloves garlic, crushed

1kg (2 pounds) minced (ground) lamb

410g (13 ounces) canned crushed tomatoes

½ cup (125ml) dry white wine

1 teaspoon ground cinnamon

¼ cup (20g) finely grated kefalotyri cheese

WHITE SAUCE

75g (2½ ounces) butter

⅓ cup (50g) plain (all-purpose) flour

2 cups (500ml) milk

1 Heat oil in large frying pan; cook eggplant, in batches, until browned both sides. Drain on absorbent paper.

2 Cook onion and garlic in same pan, stirring, until onion softens. Add lamb; cook, stirring, until lamb changes colour. Stir in undrained tomatoes, wine and cinnamon; bring to the boil. Reduce heat; simmer, uncovered, about 30 minutes or until liquid has evaporated.

3 Meanwhile, preheat oven to 180°C/350°F. Oil shallow 2-litre (8-cup) rectangular baking dish.

4 Make white sauce.

5 Place one-third of the eggplant, overlapping slices slightly, in dish; spread half the meat sauce over eggplant. Repeat layering with another third of the eggplant, remaining meat sauce and remaining eggplant. Spread white sauce over top layer of eggplant; sprinkle with cheese.

6 Bake moussaka about 40 minutes or until top browns lightly. Cover; stand 10 minutes before serving.

white sauce Melt butter in medium saucepan, add flour; cook, stirring, until mixture bubbles and thickens. Gradually add milk; stir until mixture boils and thickens.

prep + cook time 1 hour 50 minutes **serves** 6
nutritional count per serving 36.6g total fat (16.5g saturated fat); 2420kJ (579 cal); 18g carbohydrate; 41.8g protein; 5.3g fibre
tip Kefalotyri is a greek, hard, salty cheese made from sheep and/or goat's milk. Its colour varies from white to yellow depending on the mixture of milk used in the process and its age. It's great for grating over pasta or salads and can be replaced by parmesan.
serving suggestion Serve with a green salad.

rabbit

Rabbit is a lean, white meat. Historically, rabbit was commonly eaten in Australia, because it was widely available, inexpensive and highly nutritious. Although rabbit fell out of favour some time ago, it is becoming increasingly popular in contemporary Australian cooking.

Cooking rabbit

Young rabbits, classified as fryers until they are three months old, are tender with a mild flavour. The meat of mature rabbits (eight months old) is darker, firmer and stronger in flavour, and is better used in dishes which require a long, slow cooking method.

Rabbit meat is comparable in taste and texture to poultry. Its high meat to bone ratio (greater than chickens even) makes it an economical choice. Due to its low fat content, care must be taken when cooking, to prevent drying it out. Rabbit must be cooked slowly at low temperatures, or quickly in a pan. Rabbit is at its best when used in a terrine or slow-cooked dishes, like stews, casseroles and pies.

Rabbit: the healthy choice

Rabbit meat is a high-quality source of protein. It has a lower fat content than beef, pork and chicken. It has fewer calories than other popular meats. It is also low in cholesterol and sodium, making rabbit a healthy, diet-friendly choice.

Rabbit: the sustainable choice

As eating rabbit is becoming more and more popular, there is a growing number of small-scale farmers in Australia, and butchers are more frequently stocking it (usually frozen, not fresh). Rabbit is a sustainable source of meat. The environmental impact of rearing rabbits is very low, especially when compared to other farm animals. It is only three months from conception to harvesting maturity. The meat produced by one doe, a female rabbit, is comparable to that of a cow, but requires vastly less land and resources.

rabbit & hazelnut terrine

2 rabbits (1.8kg)

400g (12½ ounces) pork sausages

1 cup (250ml) red wine

3 cloves garlic, crushed

1 tablespoon finely chopped fresh thyme

½ cup (70g) hazelnuts, roasted

3 teaspoons salt

1 teaspoon freshly ground black pepper

¼ teaspoon freshly grated nutmeg

18 thin slices streaky bacon (540g)

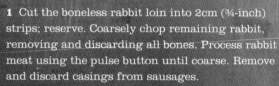

1 Cut the boneless rabbit loin into 2cm (¾-inch) strips; reserve. Coarsely chop remaining rabbit, removing and discarding all bones. Process rabbit meat using the pulse button until coarse. Remove and discard casings from sausages.

2 Combine chopped rabbit, sausage meat, wine, garlic and thyme in large bowl. Cover; refrigerate 4 hours or overnight.

3 Stir nuts, salt, pepper and nutmeg into meat mixture.

4 Preheat oven to 180°C/350°F. Line base and two long sides of 9cm x 23cm (3¾-inch x 9¼-inch) loaf pan with baking paper, extending paper 5cm (2 inches) over edges of pan. Line pan with bacon, overlapping each slice and allowing slices to overhang edges by about 4cm (1½ inches).

5 Press half the meat mixture into pan; place rabbit loin strips on top, cover with remaining meat mixture. Cover pan with foil; place pan in large baking dish, pour enough boiling water into dish to come halfway up sides of pan.

6 Bake terrine 45 minutes; remove foil, bake another 45 minutes or until cooked when tested.

7 Remove pan from dish; cover terrine with baking paper. Cool at room temperature 1 hour. Place another dish or same-sized loaf pan, filled with heavy cans on terrine to weight; refrigerate overnight. Refrigerate 2 days.

prep + cook time 2 hours (+ refrigeration & cooling)
serves 12
nutritional count per serving 17.6g total fat (5.6g saturated fat); 1278kJ (305 cal); 1.8g carbohydrate; 31.7g protein; 1.2g fibre
tip This terrine will keep tightly wrapped in plastic wrap for up to one week.
serving suggestion Serve with cornichons (baby gherkins) and crusty bread.

chicken & leek pie

2 cups (500ml) chicken stock

625g (1¼ pounds) chicken breast fillets

1 tablespoon olive oil

45g (1½ ounces) butter

1 large leek (500g), sliced thinly

2 sticks celery (300g), trimmed, chopped finely

2 tablespoons plain (all-purpose) flour

2 teaspoons fresh thyme leaves

½ cup (125ml) milk

1 cup (250ml) pouring cream

2 teaspoons wholegrain mustard

2 sheets shortcrust pastry

1 sheet puff pastry

1 egg yolk

1 Bring stock to the boil in medium saucepan. Add chicken; return to the boil. Reduce heat; simmer, covered, about 10 minutes or until chicken is cooked. Remove from heat; stand chicken in poaching liquid 10 minutes. Remove chicken; chop coarsely. Reserve 1 cup of the poaching liquid; keep remainder for another use, or discard.
2 Heat oil and butter in medium saucepan; cook leek and celery, stirring, until leek softens. Add flour and thyme; cook, stirring, 1 minute. Gradually stir in reserved poaching liquid, milk and cream; cook, stirring, until mixture boils and thickens. Stir in chicken and mustard. Cool 10 minutes.
3 Preheat oven to 200°C/400°F. Oil 1.5-litre (6-cup) ovenproof dish.
4 Line base and side of dish with shortcrust pastry, trim to fit; prick all over with fork. Bake pastry case 10 minutes. Cool 5 minutes.
5 Spoon chicken mixture into pastry case; place puff pastry over filling, trim to fit dish. Brush pastry with egg yolk; cut two small slits in top.
6 Bake pie about 20 minutes or until browned lightly.

prep + cook time 1 hour 35 minutes **serves** 6
nutritional count per serving 56g total fat (30.1g saturated fat); 3344kJ (800 cal); 42.5g carbohydrate; 31.1g protein; 3.6g fibre

meat pies

1½ cups (225g) plain (all-purpose) flour

90g (3 ounces) cold butter, chopped coarsely

1 egg

1 tablespoon iced water, approximately

2 sheets puff pastry

1 egg, extra

BEEF FILLING

1 tablespoon vegetable oil

1 small brown onion (80g), chopped finely

625g (1¼ pounds) minced (ground) beef

410g (13 ounces) canned crushed tomatoes

2 tablespoons tomato paste

2 tablespoons worcestershire sauce

¾ cup (180ml) beef stock

1 Process flour and butter until crumbly. Add egg and enough of the water to make ingredients cling together. Knead on floured surface until smooth. Wrap pastry in plastic; refrigerate 30 minutes.

2 Meanwhile, make beef filling.

3 Oil six ⅔-cup (160ml) pie tins. Divide pastry into six portions; roll each between sheets of baking paper until large enough to line tins. Lift pastry into tins; gently press over base and sides; trim. Refrigerate 30 minutes.

4 Cut six 11cm (4½-inch) rounds from puff pastry. Refrigerate until required.

5 Preheat oven to 200°C/400°F.

6 Place pastry cases on oven tray; line pastry with baking paper then fill with dried beans or uncooked rice. Bake 10 minutes; remove paper and beans. Bake a further 5 minutes; cool.

7 Fill pastry cases with beef filling; brush edges of pastry with extra egg. Top with puff pastry rounds; press edges to seal. Brush tops with egg. Cut steam holes in top of pies.

8 Bake pies about 20 minutes or until golden.

beef filling Heat oil in large saucepan, add onion and beef; cook, stirring, until beef is well browned. Stir in undrained tomatoes, paste, sauce and stock; bring to the boil. Reduce heat, simmer, uncovered, about 20 minutes or until thick. Cool.

prep + cook time 1 hour 35 minutes (+ refrigeration)
makes 6
nutritional count per pie 38.7g total fat
(13.8g saturated fat); 2876kJ (688 cal);
52.4g carbohydrate; 31.2g protein; 3.5g fibre
serving suggestion Serve with tomato sauce (ketchup).

minute-steak sandwich

2 tablespoons olive oil

1 medium brown onion (150g), sliced thinly

4 minute steaks (250g)

8 slices sourdough bread (560g), toasted

25g (¾ ounce) baby rocket (arugula) leaves

12 cornichons (baby gherkins), sliced lengthways

1 Heat oil in large frying pan over high heat; cook onion, stirring, until golden.
2 Push onion to one side of pan, add steaks; cook steaks until done to your liking.
3 Place rocket on four slices of toasted bread; top with steak, onion and cornichons. Top with remaining piece of toast.

prep + cook time 10 minutes **makes** 4
nutritional count per sandwich 15.9g total fat (3.2g saturated fat); 2452kJ (586 cal); 83.5g carbohydrate; 26.4g protein; 7.9g fibre
serving suggestion Serve with tomato chutney and chips.

peppered fillet steak with creamy bourbon sauce

4 x 125g (4 ounces) beef fillet steaks

2 teaspoons cracked black pepper

2 tablespoons olive oil

6 shallots (150g), sliced thinly

1 clove garlic, crushed

⅓ cup (80ml) bourbon

¼ cup (60ml) beef stock

2 teaspoons dijon mustard

1¼ cups (310ml) pouring cream

1 Rub beef all over with pepper. Heat half the oil in large frying pan; cook beef, uncovered, until cooked as desired. Remove from pan; cover to keep warm.
2 Heat remaining oil in same pan; cook shallot and garlic, stirring, until shallot softens. Add bourbon; stir until mixture simmers and starts to thicken. Add remaining ingredients; bring to the boil. Reduce heat; simmer, uncovered, about 5 minutes or until sauce thickens slightly.
3 Serve beef on serving plates, drizzle with sauce.

prep + cook time 20 minutes **serves** 4
nutritional count per serving 49.3g total fat (25.9g saturated fat); 2742kJ (656 cal); 13.2g carbohydrate; 28.7g protein; 0.7g fibre
tip It is fine to use just one 300ml carton of cream for this recipe.
serving suggestion Serve with fried potatoes and steamed green beans.

THE COUNTRY ROAST There's something comforting about the traditional food we associate with the country. A flavoursome roast served to the whole family, with bright garden vegetables and gravy, is a cherished Australian Sunday lunch custom.

roast chicken with tomato braised beans

2kg (4-pound) whole chicken

1 medium lemon (140g), quartered

6 sprigs fresh thyme

6 cloves garlic, unpeeled

60g (2 ounces) butter, softened

2 tablespoons lemon juice

2 cloves garlic, crushed

2 teaspoons finely chopped fresh thyme

1 cup (250ml) water

1 tablespoon olive oil

1 medium brown onion (150g), chopped coarsely

1kg (2 pounds) green beans

4 medium tomatoes (600g), chopped coarsely

1 Preheat oven to 200°C/400°F.

2 Tuck wing tips under chicken. Fill cavity with lemon, thyme sprigs and garlic, fold skin over to enclose filling; secure with toothpicks. Tie legs together with kitchen string.

3 Combine butter, juice, crushed garlic and chopped thyme in small bowl; rub butter mixture all over chicken.

4 Place chicken on oiled rack in large baking dish; pour the water into dish. Roast about 2 hours, basting occasionally with pan juices.

5 Meanwhile, heat oil in large saucepan; cook onion, stirring, until onion softens. Add beans and tomato; cook, covered, stirring occasionally, about 20 minutes or until vegetables soften slightly.

6 Serve chicken with beans.

prep + cook time 2 hours 40 minutes **serves** 6
nutritional count per serving 33.5g total fat (12.7g saturated fat); 2123kJ (508 cal); 8.3g carbohydrate; 40.3g protein; 7.3g fibre
serving suggestion Serve with roasted kipfler (fingerling) potatoes. We roasted them with the chicken for the last hour of cooking time.

roast chicken with herb stuffing

1.5kg (3-pound) whole chicken

20g (¾ ounce) butter, melted

HERB STUFFING

1½ cups (105g) stale breadcrumbs

1 stick celery (150g), trimmed, chopped finely

1 small white onion (100g), chopped finely

1 teaspoon dried mixed herbs

1 egg, beaten lightly

50g (1½ ounces) butter, melted

1 Preheat oven to 200°C/400°F.
2 Make herb stuffing.
3 Fill chicken cavity with stuffing, fold over skin to enclose; secure with toothpicks. Tie legs together with kitchen string.
4 Place chicken on rack over baking dish half-filled with water (water should not touch chicken). Brush chicken with melted butter.
5 Roast chicken 15 minutes; reduce oven to 180°C/350°F, roast further 1½ hours or until cooked through. Stand 10 minutes before serving.
herb stuffing Combine ingredients in medium bowl.

prep + cook time 2 hours 15 minutes **serves** 4
nutritional count per serving 46.8g total fat (19.4g saturated fat); 2817kJ (674 cal); 19.7g carbohydrate; 43.4g protein; 1.9g fibre
serving suggestion Serve with roasted baby new potatoes and steamed asparagus.

kangaroo

Kangaroo meat is lean and healthy. High in protein and iron and low in fat, kangaroo meat is a great alternative to more popular red meats. Kangaroo is the ultimate free-range, organic meat, containing no chemicals or antibiotics.

The Skippy dilemma

Kangaroo is becoming more commonplace in contemporary Australian cooking, frequently featuring on restaurant menus and in supermarkets. Today supermarkets stock kangaroo meat in a range of cuts, including fillets, steaks, minces and kanga bangas (sausages). Despite its increasing popularity, 70 per cent of all kangaroo meat is exported to over 55 countries. The majority of exported kangaroo meat is sent to France and Germany, where it is valued for its health benefits. As Australians we find it difficult to separate memories of Skippy or a beloved national pet, from eating a kangaroo steak.

With obesity and its associated health conditions becoming more and more prevalent, kangaroo is bound to become a more common choice for the average Australian family. A lean, high-quality source of protein, kangaroo is a diet-friendly red meat.

Cooking kangaroo

Kangaroo is easily overcooked due to the leanness of the meat (it is typically one to two per cent fat). It must be cooked carefully to prevent drying it out. Brush the meat with oil before pan-frying, barbecuing and roasting, and cook quickly on a high heat to prevent overcooking.

Sustainability

Kangaroo farming is a sustainable industry that does not threaten the species' natural population. Farming native animals is beneficial because there is no cost to the Australian environment to produce kangaroo meat.

kangaroo skewers with bagna cauda

600g (1¼ pounds) kangaroo fillet

⅔ cup (160ml) extra virgin olive oil

3 drained anchovies, chopped finely

2 cloves garlic, crushed

4 sprigs fresh thyme

2 teaspoons finely grated lemon rind

2 tablespoons lemon juice

1 Remove any sinew from kangaroo fillet; cut into 3cm (1¼-inch) cubes. Combine kangaroo with 1 tablespoon of the oil in medium bowl. Thread onto six metal skewers; season.
2 Preheat grill or barbecue flat plate on high.
3 Heat ¼ cup of the oil in large baking dish on barbecue. Add anchovies and garlic; cook, stirring, 2 minutes or until anchovies have melted and garlic is golden. Add thyme and remaining oil; stand on barbecue until warm. Remove from heat; stir in rind and juice. Season. Reserve ⅓ cup of the bagna cauda.
4 Cook skewers on heated grill (or barbecue flat plate) about 3 minutes, turning once, for rare. Add skewers to dish, turning to coat in warm bagna cauda; stand loosely covered with foil 5 minutes. Serve skewers drizzled with reserved bagna cauda.

prep + cook time 20 minutes **makes** 6
nutritional count per skewer 25.8g total fat (3.9g saturated fat); 1339kJ (320 cal); 0.3g carbohydrate; 22g protein; 0.2g fibre
tips Kangaroo meat is very lean, so it must be cooked rare to be tender. It is sold in all supermarkets. Several cuts are available but the fillet is the best for this recipe.
serving suggestion Serve with grilled asparagus, zucchini and capsicum (bell pepper).

Young, New South Wales

beef rib roast with spiced salt

1 tablespoon each coriander seeds and cumin seeds

½ cup (60g) sea salt flakes

¼ teaspoon mixed spice

1 teaspoon freshly ground pepper

3kg (6-pound) beef standing rib roast

1 tablespoon olive oil

GARLIC MAYONNAISE

1 cup (300g) whole-egg mayonnaise

1 tablespoon water

2 teaspoons lemon juice

2 cloves garlic, crushed

1 teaspoon dijon mustard

1 Preheat oven to 200°C/400°F.

2 Using a mortar and pestle, grind seeds together until coarsely crushed. Add salt, mixed spice and pepper; mix well. Remove a third of the spice mixture and reserve. Brush beef with oil, rub remaining spice mixture all over beef.

3 Roast beef, uncovered, about 1½ hours for rare, or until cooked as desired. Cover; stand 15 minutes before carving.

4 Meanwhile, dry-fry reserved spice mix in small frying pan, stirring over low heat about 1 minute or until fragrant. Cool.

5 Make garlic mayonnaise.

6 Serve beef with mayonnaise and toasted spice mix.

garlic mayonnaise Combine ingredients in small bowl.

prep + cook time 1 hour 50 minutes (+ standing)
serves 4
nutritional count per serving 62.6g total fat (18.3g saturated fat); 4468kJ (1069 cal); 14.5g carbohydrate; 112.4g protein; 0.7g fibre
serving suggestion Serve with a green salad.

roast lamb with anchovies & garlic

45g (1½ ounces) canned anchovy fillets

1.5kg (3-pound) easy carve leg of lamb

1 tablespoon fresh rosemary leaves

2 cloves garlic, sliced thinly

2 bulbs garlic, halved horizontally, extra

4 medium parsnips (500g)

2 tablespoons olive oil

500g (1 pound) asparagus

12 small truss tomatoes

¼ cup (60ml) red wine

1 tablespoon balsamic vinegar

1 cup (250ml) beef stock

1 Preheat oven to 180°C/350°F. Drain anchovies over small bowl; reserve oil. Chop anchovies coarsely.

2 Using sharp knife, pierce lamb about 12 times all over, gently twisting to make a small hole. Press anchovies, rosemary and sliced garlic evenly into holes. Place lamb on oiled wire rack in baking dish; pour reserved anchovy oil over lamb. Roast, uncovered, 1 hour 20 minutes or until lamb is cooked as desired.

3 Meanwhile, place extra garlic and parsnips in separate baking dish, drizzle with half the olive oil; roast alongside lamb 40 minutes. Add asparagus, tomatoes and remaining olive oil; roast further 10 minutes or until vegetables are tender.

4 Remove lamb from dish. Cover; stand 10 minutes.

5 Meanwhile, drain fat from dish; place dish over medium heat. Add wine; bring to the boil. Add vinegar, stock and any lamb pan juices; cook, stirring, until sauce boils and reduces to 1 cup.

6 Serve lamb with garlic, vegetables and sauce.

prep + cook time 1 hour 50 minutes **serves** 4
nutritional count per serving 25.9g total fat
(8.3g saturated fat); 2537kJ (607 cal);
16.3g carbohydrate; 70.2g protein; 8.6g fibre

roast lamb dinner

2kg (4-pound) leg of lamb

3 sprigs fresh rosemary, chopped coarsely

½ teaspoon sweet paprika

1kg (2 pounds) potatoes, chopped coarsely

500g (1 pound) pumpkin, chopped coarsely

3 medium brown onions (450g), quartered

2 tablespoons olive oil

2 tablespoons plain (all-purpose) flour

1 cup (250ml) chicken stock

¼ cup (60ml) dry red wine

1 Preheat oven to 200°C/400°F.

2 Place lamb in oiled large baking dish; using sharp knife, score skin at 2cm (¾-inch) intervals, sprinkle with rosemary and paprika. Roast lamb 15 minutes.

3 Reduce oven to 180°C/350°F; roast lamb about 45 minutes or until cooked as desired.

4 Meanwhile, place potatoes, pumpkin and onions, in single layer, in large shallow baking dish; drizzle with oil. Roast for last 45 minutes of lamb cooking time.

5 Remove lamb and vegetables from baking dish; strain pan juices from lamb into medium jug. Cover lamb and vegetables to keep warm.

6 Return ¼ cup of the pan juices to baking dish, stir in flour; stir over heat 5 minutes or until mixture bubbles and browns. Gradually add stock and wine; stir over high heat until gravy boils and thickens. Strain gravy into medium heatproof jug.

7 Serve lamb sliced with vegetables and gravy.

prep + cook time 1 hour 30 minutes **serves** 6
nutritional count per serving 21.4g total fat (8.1g saturated fat); 2372kJ (567 cal); 31.3g carbohydrate; 60g protein; 5.2g fibre

roast leg of pork with apple sauce

2.5kg (5-pound) boneless pork leg roast, rind on

2 tablespoons olive oil

1 tablespoon sea salt flakes

6 medium potatoes (1.2kg), quartered

2 tablespoons olive oil, extra

2 tablespoons each fresh sage leaves and
fresh rosemary leaves

APPLE SAUCE

3 large green apples (600g)

½ cup (125ml) water

1 teaspoon white (granulated) sugar

pinch ground cinnamon

1 Preheat oven to 220°C/425°F.

2 Score pork rind with sharp knife; tie pork at
5cm (2-inch) intervals with kitchen string. Place
pork in large shallow baking dish; rub with oil,
then salt. Roast, uncovered, 20 minutes.

3 Reduce oven to 180°C/350°F; roast pork,
uncovered, further 2 hours.

4 Meanwhile, combine potato with extra oil and
herbs in large bowl. Place in single layer on oven
tray. Roast, uncovered, about 35 minutes.

5 Make apple sauce.

6 Stand pork, covered loosely with foil, 10 minutes
before slicing. Serve pork and potatoes with sauce.

apple sauce Peel and core apples; slice thickly.
Place apples and the water in medium saucepan;
simmer, uncovered, about 10 minutes or until
apple is soft. Remove pan from heat; stir in sugar
and cinnamon.

prep + cook time 2 hours 40 minutes **serves** 8
nutritional count per serving 34g total fat
(9.7g saturated fat); 2976kJ (712 cal);
27.4g carbohydrate; 71.9g protein; 4.1g fibre
tips The three magic ingredients for crispy
savoury crackling are oil, salt and heat. Make
sure the rind is dry and rubbed well with oil and
salt. The pork must be placed in a very hot oven
for the skin to start bubbling and browning up.
Apple sauce can be made one day ahead. Store in an
airtight container or glass jar in the refrigerator.
Reheat sauce before serving. You can add a handful
of cranberries to the apples and increase the sugar
to reduce any tartness. For a brandied apple sauce,
add raisins, chopped roasted hazelnuts and a
little brandy.

orange marmalade glazed ham

7kg (14-pound) cooked leg of ham

350g (11 ounces) orange marmalade

¼ cup (55g) firmly packed light brown sugar

¼ cup (60ml) orange juice

whole cloves, to decorate

1 Preheat oven to 180°C/350°F.

2 Cut through rind of ham 10cm (4 inches) from the shank end of the leg.

3 To remove rind, run thumb around edge of rind just under skin. Start pulling rind from widest edge of ham, continue to pull rind carefully away from the fat up to the shank end. Remove rind completely. Score across the fat at about 3cm (1¼-inch) intervals, cutting lightly through the surface of the fat (not the meat) in a diamond pattern.

4 Stir marmalade, sugar and juice in small saucepan over low heat until sugar is dissolved.

5 Line large baking dish with overlapping sheets of baking paper. Place ham on wire rack in baking dish. Brush ham well with marmalade glaze; cover shank end with foil.

6 Bake ham 40 minutes. Decorate ham with cloves; bake a further 40 minutes or until browned all over, brushing occasionally with marmalade glaze during cooking.

prep + cook time 1 hour 50 minutes **serves** 10
nutritional count per serving 29.5g total fat (10.9g saturated fat); 3164kJ (757 cal); 28.7g carbohydrate; 94.9g protein; 0.3g fibre
tip This ham recipe can serve up to 12 people, depending on the rest of your menu.

PUDDINGS & DESSERTS Crumbles, puddings and pies are the desserts our grandmothers made for us, and we'll always have a soft spot for them. They're made with love and served warm from the oven.

lemon meringue pie

½ cup (75g) cornflour (cornstarch)

1 cup (220g) caster (superfine) sugar

½ cup (125ml) lemon juice

1¼ cups (310ml) water

2 teaspoons finely grated lemon rind

60g (2 ounces) unsalted butter, chopped

3 eggs, separated

½ cup (110g) caster (superfine) sugar, extra

PASTRY

1½ cups (225g) plain (all-purpose) flour

1 tablespoon icing (confectioners') sugar

140g (4½ ounces) cold butter, chopped

1 egg yolk

2 tablespoons cold water

1 Make pastry.
2 Grease 24cm (9½-inch) round loose-based fluted flan tin. Roll pastry between sheets of baking paper until large enough to line tin. Ease pastry into tin, press into base and side; trim edge. Cover; refrigerate 30 minutes.
3 Preheat oven to 240°C/475°F.
4 Place tin on oven tray. Line pastry with baking paper; fill with dried beans or rice. Bake 15 minutes. Carefully remove paper and beans; bake further 10 minutes. Cool, turn oven off.

5 Meanwhile, combine cornflour and sugar in medium saucepan; gradually stir in juice and the water until smooth. Cook, stirring, over high heat, until mixture boils and thickens. Reduce heat; simmer, stirring, 1 minute. Remove from heat; stir in rind, butter and egg yolks. Cool 10 minutes.
6 Spread lemon filling into pastry case. Cover; refrigerate 2 hours.
7 Preheat oven to 240°C/475°F.
8 Beat egg whites in small bowl with electric mixer until soft peaks form; gradually add extra sugar, beating until sugar dissolves.
9 Roughen surface of filling with fork, then spread with meringue mixture. Bake about 2 minutes or until meringue is browned lightly.
pastry Process flour, icing sugar and butter until crumbly. Add egg yolk and the water; process until ingredients come together. Knead dough on floured surface until smooth. Wrap pastry in plastic; refrigerate 30 minutes.

prep + cook time 1 hour 10 minutes (+ refrigeration)
serves 10
nutritional count per serving 18.9g total fat (11.6g saturated fat); 1772kJ (424 cal); 57.7g carbohydrate; 5g protein; 0.9g fibre
tip Roughening the surface of the filling with a fork helps prevent the meringue from shrinking away from the filling as it cooks.

chocolate self-saucing pudding

60g (2 ounces) unsalted butter

½ cup (125ml) milk

½ teaspoon vanilla extract

¾ cup (165g) caster (superfine) sugar

1 cup (150g) self-raising flour

1 tablespoon cocoa powder

¾ cup (165g) firmly packed light brown sugar

1 tablespoon cocoa powder, extra

2 cups (500ml) boiling water

1 Preheat oven to 180°C/350°F. Grease 1.5-litre (6-cup) ovenproof dish.
2 Melt butter with milk in medium saucepan. Remove from heat; stir in extract and caster sugar then sifted flour and cocoa.
3 Spread pudding mixture into dish. Sift brown sugar and extra cocoa over mixture; gently pour boiling water over mixture.
4 Bake pudding about 40 minutes or until centre is firm. Stand 5 minutes before serving.

prep + cook time 55 minutes **serves** 6
nutritional count per serving 9.7g total fat (6.2g saturated fat); 1676kJ (401 cal); 73.4g carbohydrate; 3.8g protein; 1.1g fibre

banoffee pie

395g (12½ ounces) canned sweetened condensed milk

75g (2½ ounces) unsalted butter, chopped

½ cup (110g) firmly packed light brown sugar

2 tablespoons golden syrup

1¼ cups (310ml) thickened (heavy) cream

2 large bananas (460g), sliced thinly

1 teaspoon ground nutmeg

PASTRY

1½ cups (225g) plain (all-purpose) flour

1 tablespoon icing (confectioners') sugar

140g (4½ ounces) cold butter, chopped

1 egg yolk

2 tablespoons cold water

1 Make pastry.

2 Grease 24cm (9½-inch) round loose-based fluted flan tin. Roll dough between sheets of baking paper until large enough to line tin. Ease dough into tin; press into base and side. Trim edge; prick base all over with fork. Cover; refrigerate 30 minutes.

3 Preheat oven to 200°C/400°F.

4 Place tin on oven tray; cover dough with baking paper, fill with dried beans or rice. Bake 10 minutes. Carefully remove paper and beans; bake further 10 minutes. Cool.

5 Meanwhile, combine condensed milk, butter, sugar and syrup in medium saucepan; cook, stirring, over medium heat about 10 minutes or until mixture is caramel-coloured. Stand 5 minutes. Pour caramel into pie shell; cool.

6 Beat cream in small bowl with electric mixer until soft peaks form.

7 Place banana on caramel, top with cream; sprinkle with nutmeg.

pastry Process flour, sugar and butter until crumbly; add egg yolk and water, process until ingredients come together. Knead dough on floured surface until smooth. Wrap pastry in plastic; refrigerate 30 minutes.

prep + cook time 1 hour 20 minutes (+ refrigeration)
serves 8
nutritional count per serving 42.3g total fat (27.3g saturated fat); 2973kJ (710 cal); 76.6g carbohydrate; 9.2g protein; 2g fibre
tips It is fine to use just one 300ml carton of cream for this recipe. It is believed that this dessert, originally called banoffi pie (the sound of the made-up word coming from a mix of banana and toffee), was developed by an East Sussex restaurateur in 1971.

pavlova

4 egg whites

1 cup (220g) caster (superfine) sugar

½ teaspoon vanilla extract

¾ teaspoon white vinegar

1¼ cups (310ml) thickened (heavy) cream

250g (8 ounces) strawberries, halved

125g (4 ounces) blueberries

¼ cup (60ml) passionfruit pulp

1 Preheat oven to 130°C/260°F. Line oven tray with baking paper. Mark 18cm (7¼-inch) circle on paper.

2 Beat egg whites in small bowl with electric mixer until soft peaks form; gradually add sugar, beating until sugar dissolves. Add extract and vinegar; beat until combined.

3 Spread meringue into circle on paper.

4 Bake pavlova about 1½ hours. Turn oven off; cool pavlova in oven with door ajar.

5 Beat cream in small bowl with electric mixer until soft peaks form.

6 Top pavlova with cream, berries and passionfruit.

prep + cook time 1 hour 50 minutes (+ cooling)
serves 8
nutritional count per serving 14.5g total fat
(9.5g saturated fat); 1110kJ (265 cal);
31.9g carbohydrate; 3.4g protein; 2g fibre
tip It is fine to use just one 300ml carton of cream for this recipe.

Young, New South Wales

black-and-blue berry pie

400g (12½ ounces) frozen blackberries

⅓ cup (75g) caster (superfine) sugar

2 tablespoons cornflour (cornstarch)

2 tablespoons water

250g (8 ounces) fresh blueberries

2 teaspoons finely grated lemon rind

½ teaspoon mixed spice

1 egg white

2 teaspoons demerara sugar

CUSTARD PASTRY

1½ cups (225g) plain (all-purpose) flour

¼ cup (35g) cornflour (cornstarch)

¼ cup (30g) custard powder

2 tablespoons icing (confectioners') sugar

125g (4 ounces) cold butter, chopped coarsely

1 egg yolk

1 tablespoon iced water, approximately

1 Make custard pastry.

2 Meanwhile, combine 1 cup of the blackberries and sugar in medium saucepan; bring to the boil. Blend cornflour with the water in small jug; pour into berry mixture, stirring over heat until mixture boils and thickens. Cool. Stir in remaining blackberries, blueberries, rind and spice.

3 Roll two-thirds of the pastry between sheets of baking paper until large enough to line 24cm (9½-inch) round loose-based flan tin. Ease pastry into tin; trim edge. Reserve and refrigerate excess pastry. Refrigerate pastry case 30 minutes.

4 Preheat oven to 200°C/400°F.

5 Spoon filling into pastry case. Brush pastry edge with egg white. Roll reserved pastry between sheets of baking paper until large enough to cover pie. Cut into 10 x 1.5cm (½-inch) strips. Place strips over pie, weaving in and out to make lattice pattern. Trim edges, pressing to seal; sprinkle with demerara sugar.

6 Bake pie about 50 minutes or until browned. Stand 10 minutes before serving.

custard pastry Process flours, custard powder, icing sugar and butter until crumbly. Add egg yolk and enough of the water until ingredients just come together. Knead pastry on floured surface until smooth. Wrap pastry in plastic; refrigerate 30 minutes.

prep + cook time 1 hour 15 minutes (+ refrigeration & cooling) **serves** 8
nutritional count per serving 14g total fat (8.7g saturated fat); 1471kJ (352 cal); 49.9g carbohydrate; 4.9g protein; 4.8g fibre

raspberry almond crumble tart

1½ cups (225g) frozen raspberries

1 teaspoon icing (confectioners') sugar

ALMOND CRUMBLE PASTRY

150g (5 ounces) butter, softened

1 teaspoon vanilla extract

⅔ cup (150g) caster (superfine) sugar

1 egg

½ cup (60g) ground almonds

1½ cups (225g) plain (all-purpose) flour

1 Make almond crumble pastry.

2 Roll two-thirds of the pastry between sheets of baking paper until large enough to line 11cm x 35cm (4½-inch x 14-inch) rectangular loose-based flan tin. Lift pastry into tin, press into base and sides; trim edge. Prick pastry base with fork; refrigerate 30 minutes. Reserve remaining pastry.

3 Meanwhile, preheat oven to 200°C/400°F.

4 Place tin on oven tray; bake, about 10 minutes or until browned lightly.

5 Sprinkle raspberries over pastry base, sprinkle with remaining crumbled pastry. Bake further 20 minutes or until well browned; cool in pan.

6 Dust with sifted icing sugar before serving.

almond crumble pastry Beat butter in small bowl with electric mixer until smooth. Add extract, sugar and egg; beat until combined. Stir in ground almonds and half the flour. Work in remaining flour using hand. Knead pastry on floured surface until smooth. Wrap pastry in plastic; refrigerate 30 minutes.

prep + cook time 1 hour (+ refrigeration & cooling)
serves 8
nutritional count per serving 20.6g total fat (10.7g saturated fat); 1576kJ (377 cal); 41.5g carbohydrate; 5.8g protein; 3.2g fibre
tip This recipe is best made on day of serving as the raspberries will soften the pastry.
serving suggestion Serve with thick (double) cream, ice-cream or custard.

bread & butter pudding

6 slices white bread (270g)

40g (1½ ounces) unsalted butter, softened

½ cup (80g) sultanas

¼ teaspoon ground nutmeg

CUSTARD

1½ cups (375ml) milk

2 cups (500ml) pouring cream

⅓ cup (75g) caster (superfine) sugar

1 teaspoon vanilla extract

4 eggs

1 Preheat oven to 160°C/325°F. Grease shallow 2-litre (8-cup) ovenproof dish.

2 Make custard.

3 Trim crusts from bread. Spread each slice with butter; cut into four triangles. Layer bread, overlapping, in dish; sprinkle with sultanas. Pour custard over bread; sprinkle with nutmeg.

4 Place ovenproof dish in large baking dish; add enough boiling water to come halfway up side of ovenproof dish. Bake about 45 minutes or until pudding is set. Remove pudding from baking dish; stand 5 minutes before serving. Serve dusted with sifted icing sugar, if you like.

custard Bring milk, cream, sugar and extract to the boil in medium saucepan. Whisk eggs in large bowl; whisking constantly, gradually add hot milk mixture to egg mixture.

prep + cook time 1 hour 15 minutes **serves** 6
nutritional count per serving 48.6g total fat (30.4g saturated fat); 2859kJ (684 cal); 49.3g carbohydrate; 12.4g protein; 1.8g fibre
tips You could use brioche or croissants instead of sliced bread for an even more luxurious version of this classic dessert. Berries, especially raspberries, also make a delicious addition.

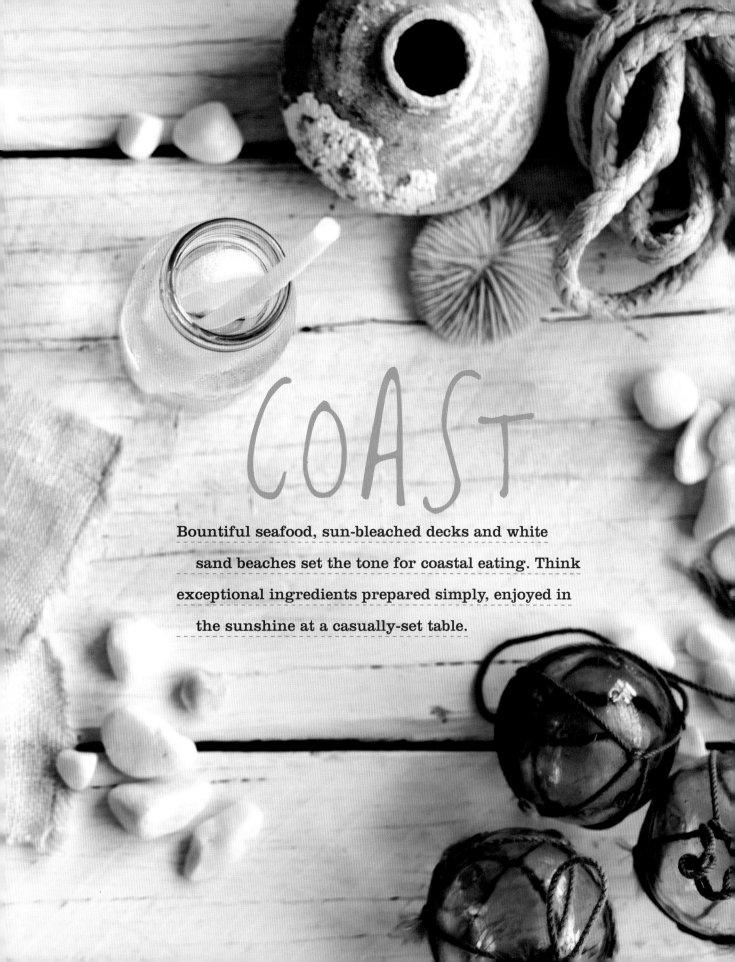

COAST

Bountiful seafood, sun-bleached decks and white sand beaches set the tone for coastal eating. Think exceptional ingredients prepared simply, enjoyed in the sunshine at a casually-set table.

COCKTAILS AT SUNDOWN Fresh from the shower after a day at the beach, nothing feels more like holidays than cocktails and a plate of oysters. Relax before dinner and enjoy.

watermelon cosmo

1 cup ice cubes

45ml (1½ fluid ounces) vodka

30ml (1 fluid ounce) triple sec

¼ cup (60ml) chilled watermelon juice

20ml (¾ fluid ounce) lime juice

1 Place ice cubes, vodka, triple sec and juices in cocktail shaker; shake vigorously.
2 Strain into chilled 230ml (7-fluid ounce) martini glass. Garnish with watermelon slices and lime peel.

prep time 5 minutes **serves** 1
nutritional count per serving 0.2g total fat (0g saturated fat); 895kJ (214 cal); 14.4g carbohydrate; 0.4g protein; 0g fibre

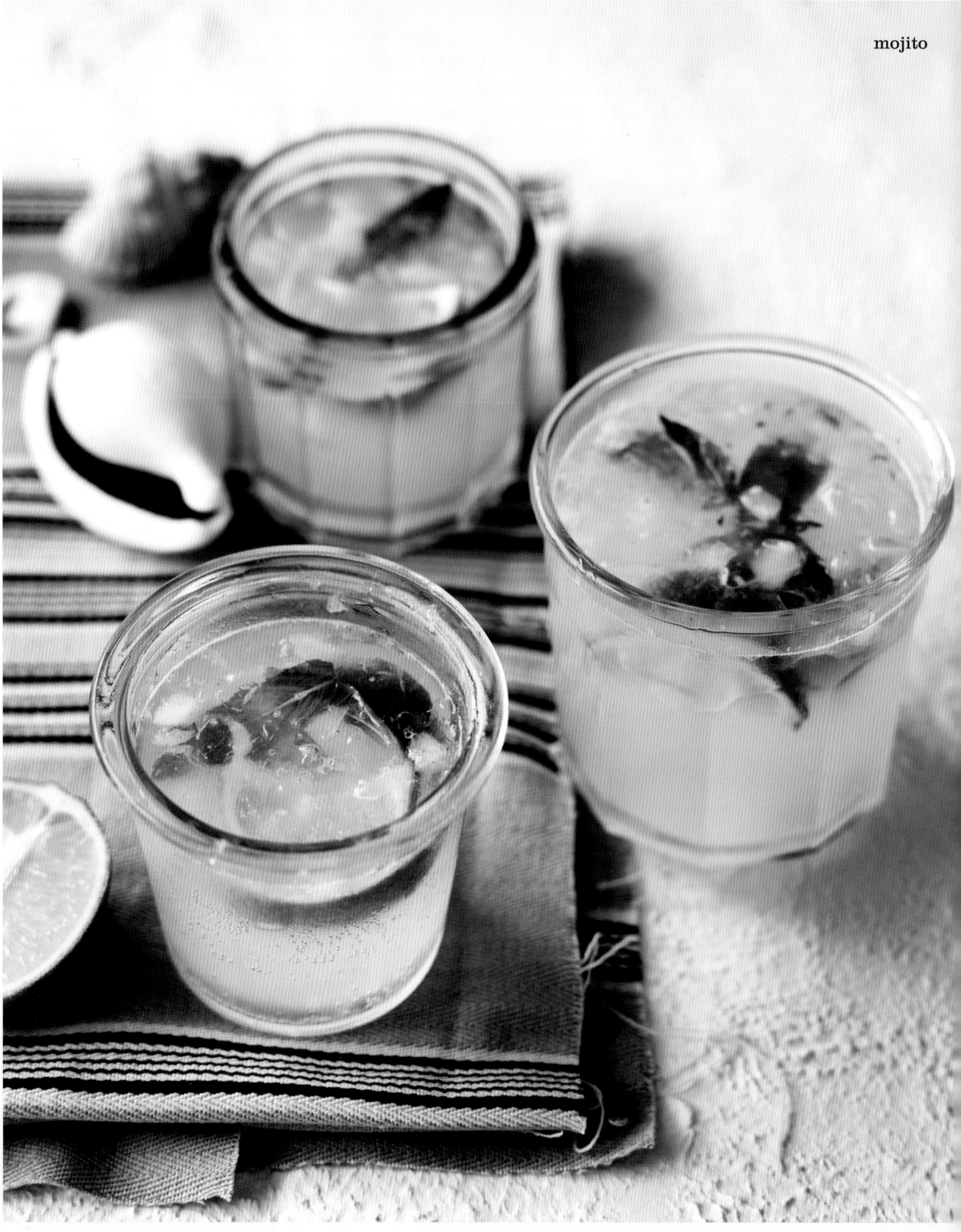

mojito

2 limes

30ml (1 fluid ounce) sugar syrup (see tip)

12 sprigs fresh mint

90ml (3 fluid ounces) white rum

1 cup ice cubes

1⅓ cups (330ml) soda water

fresh mint leaves, extra

1 Cut lime into quarters; place 6 lime wedges into cocktail shaker. Using muddler, crush lime wedges with sugar syrup and sprigs of mint. Add rum and ice; shake vigorously.
2 Strain into four 125ml (4-fluid ounce) glasses; top with soda water. Add remaining lime wedges and extra mint leaves to glass.

prep time 5 minutes **serves** 4
nutritional count per serving 0g total fat
(0g saturated fat); 196kJ (47 cal); 0g carbohydrate; 0g protein; 0g fibre
tip You can buy sugar syrup from liquor stores or make your own. Stir 1 cup caster (superfine) sugar with 1 cup water in small saucepan, over low heat, until sugar dissolves; bring to the boil. Reduce heat; simmer, uncovered, without stirring, 5 minutes. Remove from heat; cool to room temperature. Store in an airtight container in the fridge for up to 1 month.

classic margarita

2 limes, halved

2 tablespoons salt

1 cup ice cubes

45ml (1½ fluid ounces) dark tequila

30ml (1 fluid ounce) Cointreau

30ml (1 fluid ounce) sugar syrup (see tip)

1 Rub cut side of one lime half around rim of a margarita glass; turn glass upside-down and dip wet rim into saucer of salt.
2 Juice limes (you need 30ml/1 fluid ounce of juice).
3 Place ice cubes, tequila, Cointreau, sugar syrup and juice in cocktail shaker; shake vigorously.
4 Strain into glass. Garnish with slices of lime.

prep time 5 minutes **serves** 1
nutritional count per serving 0.2g total fat
(0g saturated fat); 1216kJ (291 cal);
31.4g carbohydrate; 0.3g protein; 0.1g fibre
tip You can buy sugar syrup from liquor stores or make your own. Stir 1 cup caster (superfine) sugar with 1 cup water in small saucepan, over low heat, until sugar dissolves; bring to the boil. Reduce heat; simmer, uncovered, without stirring, 5 minutes. Remove from heat; cool to room temperature. Store in an airtight container in the fridge for up to 1 month.

{photograph page 236}

classic margarita {recipe page 235}

cool as a cucumber {recipe page 238}

cool as a cucumber

⅓ cup coarsely chopped unpeeled cucumber

45ml (1½ fluid ounces) gin

30ml (1 fluid ounce) lemon juice

3 teaspoons sugar syrup (see tip)

1 cup crushed ice

1 Place chopped cucumber into cocktail shaker. Using muddler, crush cucumber. Add gin, juice, sugar syrup and ice; shake vigorously.
2 Strain into chilled 120ml (4-fluid ounce) martini glass. Garnish with extra cucumber slices.

prep time 5 minutes **serves** 1
nutritional count per serving 0.1g total fat (0g saturated fat); 564kJ (135 cal); 8.9g carbohydrate; 0.9g protein; 1.2g fibre
tip You can buy sugar syrup from liquor stores or make your own. Stir 1 cup caster (superfine) sugar with 1 cup water in small saucepan, over low heat, until sugar dissolves; bring to the boil. Reduce heat; simmer, uncovered, without stirring, 5 minutes. Remove from heat; cool to room temperature. Store in an airtight container in the fridge for up to 1 month.

{photograph page 237}

oysters with two dressings

48 oysters, on the half shell

RED WINE VINEGAR DRESSING

1 tablespoon finely chopped shallots

2 tablespoons red wine vinegar

2 teaspoons extra virgin olive oil

SPICY LIME DRESSING

2 tablespoons lime juice

2 tablespoons japanese soy sauce

1 teaspoon white (granulated) sugar

1 fresh small red thai (serrano) chilli, chopped finely

1 Make red wine vinegar dressing.
2 Make spicy lime dressing.
3 Just before serving, drizzle half the oysters with red wine vinegar dressing and the remaining oysters with spicy lime dressing.
red wine vinegar dressing Place ingredients in screw-top jar; shake well. Season to taste.
spicy lime dressing Place ingredients in screw-top jar; shake well. Season to taste.

prep time 10 minutes **makes** 48
nutritional count per oyster 0.8g total fat (0.2g saturated fat); 84kJ (20 cal); 0.3g carbohydrate; 3g protein; 0g fibre
tip Oysters are ideally served on a bed of crushed ice (especially in the summer), or nestled on a platter with a bed of rock salt to prevent them sliding around. If you don't want to serve oysters on the half shell, place single oysters on chinese soup spoons then top them with the dressings.

oysters with two dressings

BRUNCH A sleep-in, a salt-water swim, then a leisurely brunch with friends and family – we can't think of a nicer way to spend a weekend morning.

oyster shooters

1 stick celery (150g)

2¼ cups (560ml) tomato juice, chilled

1 tablespoon lemon juice

1 tablespoon worcestershire sauce

10 drops Tabasco sauce

1 cup ice cubes

8 fresh oysters

1 Cut celery into sticks long enough to use as stirrers in the shot glasses.
2 Blend or process juices, sauces and ice until smooth; refrigerate until ready to serve.
3 Divide oysters into eight shot glasses, top with tomato juice mixture; add celery sticks for stirring.

prep time 10 minutes **serves** 8
nutritional count per serving 0.4g total fat (0.1g saturated fat); 138kJ (33 cal); 4.2g carbohydrate; 2.5g protein; 0.7g fibre

green grape & apple spritzer

500g (1 pound) seedless green grapes

1 large apple (200g), chopped coarsely

2 cups (500ml) soda water, chilled

1 lime, sliced thinly

1 Using electric juicer, extract juice from grapes and apple.
2 Combine juice with soda water and lime in large jug.

prep time 10 minutes **serves** 4
nutritional count per serving 0.2g total fat (0g saturated fat); 410kJ (98 cal); 22.3g carbohydrate; 0.9g protein; 2.3g fibre

smoked salmon rösti stacks

800g (1½ pounds) medium potatoes, unpeeled, washed

⅓ cup (80ml) buttermilk

1 tablespoon prepared horseradish

1 tablespoon finely chopped fresh flat-leaf parsley

2 tablespoons olive oil

100g (3 ounces) smoked salmon slices

40g (1½ ounces) baby rocket (arugula) leaves

1 Boil, steam or microwave whole potatoes 5 minutes; drain. Cool 20 minutes.
2 Meanwhile, combine buttermilk, horseradish and parsley in small bowl.
3 Coarsely grate potatoes into medium bowl.
4 Heat oil in large frying pan; drop ¼ cups grated potato into pan, flatten with spatula. Cook rösti, in batches, until browned both sides. Remove from pan.
5 Layer rösti, salmon and rocket on serving plates; serve with buttermilk dressing.

prep + cook time 40 minutes (+ cooling) **serves** 4
nutritional count per serving 11.5g total fat (2.1g saturated fat); 1141kJ (273 cal); 28.3g carbohydrate; 11.8g protein; 4.3g fibre

{photograph page 246}

smoked salmon rösti stacks {recipe page 245}

glazed fig bruschetta {recipe page 248}

glazed fig bruschetta

6 medium fresh figs (360g), halved

2 tablespoons honey

⅔ cup (160ml) thickened (heavy) cream

1 tablespoon icing (confectioners') sugar

⅓ cup (85g) mascarpone cheese

4 thick slices brioche (150g), toasted

2 tablespoons honey, extra

1 Drizzle cut-sides of figs with honey. Place figs, cut-side down, in heated large frying pan; cook until figs are warmed through. Add 1 tablespoon cold water to pan; remove from heat.
2 Meanwhile, beat cream and sifted icing sugar in small bowl with electric mixer until soft peaks form; beat in mascarpone.
3 Spread one side of each slice of brioche with mascarpone mixture, top with fig halves; drizzle with extra honey.

prep + cook time 10 minutes **serves** 4
nutritional count per serving 31.8g total fat (19.8g saturated fat); 2137kJ (511 cal); 53.1g carbohydrate; 5.6g protein; 3g fibre

{photograph page 247}

potato & bacon pizza

2 x 335g (10½-ounce) pizza bases

2 tablespoons olive oil

4 rindless bacon slices (260g), chopped coarsely

2 cloves garlic, sliced thinly

1 tablespoon coarsely chopped fresh rosemary

½ teaspoon dried chilli flakes

500g (1 pound) potatoes, sliced thinly

1 cup (80g) finely grated parmesan cheese

1 Preheat oven to 220°C/425°F.
2 Place pizza bases on oven trays; bake about 10 minutes or until crisp.
3 Meanwhile, heat oil in large frying pan; cook bacon, garlic, rosemary and chilli, stirring, 5 minutes. Remove mixture from pan.
4 Cook potato in same heated pan, stirring frequently, about 10 minutes or until tender.
5 Sprinkle each pizza base with ⅓ cup of the cheese. Divide bacon mixture and potato between bases; top with remaining cheese.
6 Bake pizzas about 5 minutes or until browned lightly; season to taste.

prep + cook time 35 minutes **serves** 4
nutritional count per serving 25.7g total fat (7.6g saturated fat); 3486kJ (834 cal); 105.6g carbohydrate; 39.6g protein; 9g fibre
tips We used 25cm (10-inch) diameter, packaged pizza bases for this recipe. Make sure you slice the potatoes as thinly as possible.

potato & bacon pizza

SALADS & LIGHT MEALS Warmer weather invites light, zesty flavours and fuss-free mealtimes. Pile platters with salads and seafood and let everyone help themselves.

salade composé

1 small french bread stick (150g)

2 cloves garlic, crushed

¼ cup (60ml) olive oil

6 rindless bacon slices (480g), sliced thickly

150g (4½ ounces) mesclun

6 medium egg tomatoes (450g), sliced thinly

4 hard-boiled eggs, halved lengthways

RED WINE VINAIGRETTE

¼ cup (60ml) red wine vinegar

3 teaspoons dijon mustard

⅓ cup (80ml) extra virgin olive oil

1 Preheat grill (broiler).
2 Cut bread into 1cm (½-inch) slices. Brush both sides with combined garlic and oil; toast under preheated grill.
3 Cook bacon in large frying pan until crisp; drain on absorbent paper.
4 Meanwhile, make red wine vinaigrette.
5 Layer bread and bacon in large bowl with mesclun and tomato, top with egg; drizzle with vinaigrette.
red wine vinaigrette Place ingredients in screw-top jar; shake well.

prep + cook time 35 minutes **serves** 4
nutritional count per serving 51.8g total fat (11.1g saturated fat); 2859kJ (684 cal); 23.4g carbohydrate; 30.5g protein; 3.9g fibre
tip Literally meaning "composed salad", the ingredients in this dish are layered on top of each other, rather than being tossed together, and the dressing is drizzled over the top.

prawn & pesto linguine

375g (12 ounces) linguine pasta

500g (1 pound) uncooked shelled large prawns (shrimp), tails intact

2 cloves garlic, crushed

1 fresh long red (serrano) chilli, sliced thinly

1 medium zucchini (120g), cut into ribbons

180g (6 ounces) bottled chunky basil pesto dip

1 Cook pasta in large saucepan of boiling water until tender; drain, reserving ⅓ cup cooking liquid. Return pasta to pan.
2 Meanwhile, heat oiled large frying pan; cook prawns until changed in colour. Add garlic, chilli and zucchini to pan; cook until zucchini softens.
3 Add pesto, prawn mixture and reserved cooking liquid to pasta; toss gently.

prep + cook time 10 minutes **serves** 4
nutritional count per serving 19.8g total fat (4.2g saturated fat); 2571kJ (615 cal); 65.1g carbohydrate; 40.9g protein; 4.9g fibre
tip Use a vegetable peeler to cut the zucchini into ribbons.
serving suggestion We topped this dish with grated parmesan cheese, however not everyone likes to serve cheese with seafood.

ruby grapefruit, pomegranate & endive salad

3 ruby red grapefruit (1kg)

¼ cup (60ml) olive oil

2 tablespoons coarsely chopped fresh chervil

100g (3 ounces) curly endive leaves

½ cup (125ml) pomegranate pulp

½ cup (55g) coarsely chopped walnuts, roasted

1 Juice half of one grapefruit; reserve juice. Peel remaining grapefruit; slice thickly.
2 Place reserved juice in screw-top jar with oil and chervil; shake well.
3 Place endive in large bowl with dressing; toss gently to combine. Season to taste.
4 Arrange endive, grapefruit and pomegranate on serving plate; sprinkle with nuts.

prep time 15 minutes **serves** 4
nutritional count per serving 23.7g total fat (2.5g saturated fat); 1208kJ (289 cal); 12.8g carbohydrate; 4.5g protein; 4.6g fibre
tip You need 1 medium pomegranate for this recipe. Pomegranate pulp consists of the seeds and the edible pulp surrounding them; it has a tangy sweet-sour flavour. To remove the seeds, cut the fruit in half crossways and hold each half cut-side down over a bowl. Hit the outside skin of the fruit sharply with a wooden spoon – as hard as you can – the seeds should fall out – if they don't, dig them out with a teaspoon.

tomato & rocket tarts

tomato & rocket tarts

2 sheets shortcrust pastry

250g (8 ounces) baby tomatoes, sliced

50g (1½ ounces) baby rocket (arugula) leaves

1½ tablespoons balsamic dressing

1 Preheat oven to 180°C/350°F. Line oven trays with baking paper.
2 Cut pastry sheets into four squares each; place on trays. Fold edges of pastry over to form a 5mm (¼-inch) border; prick pastry bases with fork
3 Bake pastry about 15 minutes or until crisp.
4 Combine tomatoes, rocket and dressing in large bowl. Spoon tomato mixture onto warm pastries.
5 Serve tarts drizzled with a little extra balsamic vinegar, if you like.

prep + cook time 20 minutes **makes** 8
nutritional count per tart 12.7g total fat
(6.2g saturated fat); 861kJ (206 cal);
19.6g carbohydrate; 3g protein; 1.4g fibre

fish sandwiches with caesar dressing

4 x 110g (3½-ounce) white fish fillets, halved

8 slices sourdough bread (560g)

1 baby cos (romaine) lettuce (180g),
leaves separated

4 hard-boiled eggs, sliced thinly

⅓ cup (25g) flaked parmesan cheese

CAESAR DRESSING

½ cup (125ml) buttermilk

1 tablespoon whole-egg mayonnaise

2 teaspoons red wine vinegar

4 drained anchovy fillets, chopped finely

1 Make caesar dressing.
2 Cook fish in heated oiled frying pan until cooked through. Remove from heat, cover fish; stand 5 minutes.
3 Spread bread slices with dressing; sandwich lettuce, egg, fish, cheese and remaining dressing between bread slices.
caesar dressing Place ingredients in screw-top jar; shake well.

prep + cook time 25 minutes **makes** 4
nutritional count per roll 18.3g total fat
(5.1g saturated fat); 2588kJ (618 cal);
65.9g carbohydrate; 46.6g protein; 7.4g fibre
tip You can replace the fish with pan-fried chicken schnitzel, if you like.

{photograph page 259}

fish sandwiches with caesar dressing
{recipe page 257}

mud crab

Mud crabs are large with a smooth broad carapace and mottled blue-green shell. Native to Queensland, they live on the muddy floor of shallow coastal mangroves. Available all year, mud crabs are at their peak from January to April. Be mindful that quality can vary with the seasons.

Buying mud crabs

Mud crabs are expensive compared to other crabs, but the moist meat found in the body and claws of the mud crab has a distinct sweet flavour that is simply divine. They also have a stronger flavour and denser texture than other crabs.

Most commonly, mud crabs are sold live due to their ability to survive out of water for days. Although the claws are tied for safety, live mud crabs must be handled with care as their large claws can inflict serious injuries. Look for vigorous mud crabs that feel heavy for their size, and whose legs and claws are intact.

It is possible also to buy cooked mud crab meat. It is not recommended, however, to buy dead uncooked crabs, as it is very difficult to determine quality and freshness. If it is unavoidable, gently shake the crabs to ensure there is no water sloshing around in the shell.

Cooking mud crabs

As with any live animal, it is important to treat mud crabs humanely before cooking them. Never put live mud crabs directly into boiling water. Not only is it extremely cruel but the meat will toughen and their legs and claws can fall off.

Before cooking, put live crabs in the freezer for 45 minutes to an hour. The crabs will go to sleep but not freeze. When the crab is insensible drop it straight into rapidly boiling water or split with a sharp knife through the nerve centre, the centreline of the head and the thorax (the area between the head and the abdomen).

Mud crabs are best when cooked simply- steamed, boiled or poached in salted water (25g of salt to a litre of water), and married with classic flavours that will not overwhelm their sweet, delicate flavour. Deliciously moist, but not oily, mud crab meat turns from translucent to off-white when cooked. The recovery rate (or flesh to shell ratio) is around 25 per cent. Their impressive shells and ornate claws look spectacular on the table.

Storing mud crabs

Store live crabs in a container covered with a thick damp cloth, ensuring that the cloth does not dry out. Cooked crabs should be wrapped in plastic or stored in an airtight container for up to two days in the refrigerator.

crab & green mango salad

125g (4 ounces) bean thread noodles

2 green mangoes (700g), cut into matchsticks

300g (9½ ounces) cooked crab meat, flaked

1 small red onion (100g), sliced thinly

100g (3 ounces) baby mizuna leaves

1 cup firmly packed fresh coriander
(cilantro) leaves

SWEET CHILLI DRESSING

⅓ cup (80ml) lime juice

2 tablespoons fish sauce

2 tablespoons sweet chilli sauce

1 tablespoon grated palm sugar

1 Place noodles in medium heatproof bowl,
cover with boiling water; stand until tender,
drain. Rinse under cold water; drain.
2 Meanwhile, make sweet chilli dressing.
3 Place noodles and dressing in large bowl
with mango, crab, onion, mizuna and coriander;
toss gently to combine.
sweet chilli dressing Place ingredients in
screw-top jar, season to taste; shake well.

prep + cook time 20 minutes **serves** 4
nutritional count per serving 1.4g total fat
(0.1g saturated fat); 953kJ (228 cal);
37.2g carbohydrate; 14g protein; 3.9g fibre
tip Crab meat is available from fish markets and
the seafood section of some major supermarkets.

roquefort & witlof salad

3 witlof (belgian endive) (375g), leaves separated

1 bunch baby endive (250g), leaves separated

80g (2½ ounces) mini toasts, crushed lightly

150g (4½ ounces) roquefort cheese, crumbled

DIJON DRESSING

1 tablespoon dijon mustard

¼ cup (60ml) white wine vinegar

¼ cup (60ml) olive oil

pinch caster (superfine) sugar

1 tablespoon water

1 Make dijon dressing.
2 Place witlof, endive, toast and cheese in large bowl; toss gently to combine. Drizzle with dressing.
dijon dressing Place ingredients in screw-top jar; shake well.

prep time 10 minutes **serves** 8
nutritional count per serving 13.3g total fat (4.9g saturated fat); 711kJ (170 cal); 6.2g carbohydrate; 5.6g protein; 1.7g fibre
tip Mini toasts are available from most major supermarkets and delicatessens.

rocket, chilli & lemon spaghetti

⅓ cup (80ml) lemon-infused olive oil

1 fresh long red chilli, chopped finely

375g (12 ounces) spaghetti

80g (2½ ounces) baby rocket (arugula) leaves

1 Combine oil and chilli in small frying pan; heat gently, about 8 minutes or until hot.
2 Meanwhile, cook pasta in large saucepan of boiling water until tender. Drain, reserving ⅓ cup of the cooking liquid.
3 Return pasta to pan with chilli oil, reserved cooking liquid and rocket; stir gently to combine. Season to taste.

prep + cook time 15 minutes **serves** 4
nutritional count per serving 19.4g total fat (2.8g saturated fat); 2031kJ (486 cal); 64.6g carbohydrate; 11.2g protein; 3.6g fibre
tip You could use garlic-infused olive oil instead of the lemon-infused oil in this recipe.
serving suggestion Serve with lemon cheeks and grated parmesan cheese.

avocado caprese salad

4 large vine-ripened tomatoes (480g)

250g (8 ounces) cherry bocconcini cheese

1 large avocado (320g), halved

¼ cup loosely packed fresh basil leaves

2 tablespoons olive oil

1 tablespoon balsamic vinegar

1 Slice tomato, cheese and avocado thickly.

2 Arrange tomato, cheese and avocado on serving platter; top with basil leaves, drizzle with combined oil and vinegar. Sprinkle with freshly ground black pepper, if you like.

prep time 10 minutes **serves** 4
nutritional count per serving 29g total fat (10.1g saturated fat); 1342kJ (321 cal); 2.3g carbohydrate; 13.1g protein; 2.3g fibre
tip We used vine-ripened truss tomatoes because it takes a simple recipe like this for their brilliant colour, robust flavour and crisp, tangy flesh to stand out at their magnificent best. Use less costly tomatoes to cook with, but always go for these when you're serving them raw.

salad niçoise

200g (6½ ounces) green beans, trimmed, halved

1 small red onion (100g), sliced thinly

4 medium egg tomatoes (600g), seeded, cut into thin wedges

3 hard-boiled eggs, quartered

425g (13½ ounces) canned tuna in spring water, drained, flaked

⅓ cup (40g) seeded small black olives

⅓ cup (55g) drained caperberries, rinsed

2 tablespoons finely shredded fresh basil

1 tablespoon coarsely chopped fresh flat-leaf parsley

DRESSING

2 tablespoons olive oil

2 tablespoons white wine vinegar

1 tablespoon lemon juice

1 Boil, steam or microwave beans until tender; drain. Rinse under cold water; drain.
2 Make dressing.
3 Place beans in large bowl with dressing and remaining ingredients; toss gently to combine.
dressing Place ingredients in screw-top jar; shake well.

prep + cook time 20 minutes **serves** 4
nutritional count per serving 16g total fat (3.5g saturated fat); 1292kJ (309 cal); 9.6g carbohydrate; 29.6g protein; 4.2g fibre

roasted capsicum & goat's cheese salad

2 medium orange capsicums (bell peppers) (400g)

2 medium red capsicums (bell peppers) (400g)

2 medium yellow capsicums (bell peppers) (400g)

2 medium green capsicums (bell peppers) (400g)

80g (2½ ounces) baby rocket (arugula) leaves

1 small red onion (100g), sliced thinly

240g (7½ ounces) goat's cheese, crumbled

OREGANO VINAIGRETTE

⅓ cup (80ml) olive oil

2 tablespoons red wine vinegar

1 clove garlic, crushed

1 tablespoon finely chopped fresh oregano

1 Preheat oven to 200°C/400°F.

2 Quarter capsicums; discard seeds and membranes. Place, skin-side up, on oven tray. Roast 20 minutes or until skin blisters and blackens. Cover capsicum pieces with plastic or paper 5 minutes; peel away skin, then slice capsicum thickly.

3 Make oregano vinaigrette.

4 Place capsicum in large bowl with rocket and onion; toss gently to combine. Sprinkle with cheese, drizzle with vinaigrette.

oregano vinaigrette Place ingredients in screw-top jar; shake well. Season to taste.

prep + cook time 30 minutes **serves** 4
nutritional count per serving 28.5g total fat (8.8g saturated fat); 1605kJ (384 cal); 15.9g carbohydrate; 14.2g protein; 4.6g fibre

chicken & mango salad

100g (3½ ounces) mixed salad leaves

1½ cups (240g) shredded barbecued chicken

2 medium mangoes (860g), sliced thinly

DRESSING

¼ cup (60ml) lime juice

1 tablespoon finely chopped fresh coriander (cilantro)

1 fresh small red thai (serrano) chilli, chopped finely

2 teaspoons light soy sauce

1 Make dressing.

2 Place salad leaves, chicken, mango and dressing in large bowl; toss gently to combine. Season.

dressing Place ingredients in screw-top jar; shake well. Season to taste.

prep time 10 minutes **serves** 4
nutritional count per serving 5.6g total fat (1.5g saturated fat); 885kJ (211 cal); 20.7g carbohydrate; 18.8g protein; 2.4g fibre
tip You need half a barbecued chicken weighing about 450g (14½ ounces) for this amount of shredded chicken.

SEAFOOD It's an Australian custom to eat seafood in summer, and we'd be mad not to, especially if we're close to the sea. Prawns, scallops, fish and oysters – a feast of freshness.

fish steaks with kalamata olive dressing

4 x 200g (6½-ounce) white fish steaks

2 teaspoons olive oil

1 cup coarsely chopped fresh flat-leaf parsley

KALAMATA OLIVE DRESSING

1 medium red onion (170g), sliced thinly

1 cup (150g) seeded kalamata olives, chopped coarsely

8 white anchovy fillets (20g), drained, sliced thinly lengthways

1 tablespoon rigani

1 clove garlic, crushed

¼ cup (60ml) olive oil

¼ cup (60ml) red wine vinegar

1 Make kalamata olive dressing.
2 Brush steaks with oil; season. Cook steaks on heated grill plate (or grill or barbecue or grill pan) until cooked through.
3 Meanwhile, warm dressing in small saucepan; stir in parsley.
4 Serve fish steaks drizzled with dressing.
kalamata olive dressing Combine ingredients in medium bowl; season.

prep + cook time 20 minutes **serves** 4
nutritional count per serving 26g total fat (4.1g saturated fat); 1250kJ (299 cal); 2.9g carbohydrate; 13.1g protein; 2.9g fibre
tips We used swordfish in this recipe; tuna steaks and firm white fish cutlets would also be fine. The dressing can be made a day ahead, cover, store in the refrigerator.
serving suggestion Serve with garlic and lemon fried potato slices.

poached fish fillets
with herb & pea salad

4 x 200g (6½-ounce) white fish fillets,
skin removed

10cm (4-inch) stick fresh lemon grass (20g),
halved lengthways

1 lime, sliced thickly

HERB & PEA SALAD

100g (3 ounces) snow peas, sliced finely

150g (4½ ounces) sugar snap peas

50g (1½ ounces) baby asian greens

½ cup loosely packed fresh coriander
(cilantro) leaves

⅓ cup each loosely packed fresh vietnamese mint
leaves, mint leaves and dill sprigs

ASIAN DRESSING

¼ cup (60ml) lime juice

2 tablespoons fish sauce

2 teaspoons peanut oil

2 teaspoons grated palm sugar

1 fresh small red thai (serrano) chilli,
chopped finely

1 clove garlic, chopped finely

1 Place fish, lemon grass and lime in large frying pan; barely cover fish with cold water. Bring slowly to a gentle simmer. Remove from heat; stand pan, covered, 10 minutes. Remove fish from liquid; drain.
2 Meanwhile, make herb & pea salad, then asian dressing. Add half the dressing to the salad; toss gently to combine.
3 Serve fish topped with salad; drizzle with remaining dressing.
herb & pea salad Combine ingredients in medium bowl.
asian dressing Place ingredients in screw-top jar; shake well.

prep + cook time 35 minutes **serves** 4
nutritional count per serving 6.1g total fat
(1.6g saturated fat); 942kJ (225 cal);
5.9g carbohydrate; 36.1g protein; 3.3g fibre
tips Vietnamese mint is not actually mint, but a pungent and peppery narrow-leafed member of the buckwheat family. Also known as laksa leaf and cambodian mint, it is available from Asian greengrocers. We used blue-eye trevalla cutlets in this recipe, but you can use any white fish cutlets.

salmon

Tasmanian Atlantic salmon has an international reputation for superior quality and taste. Although not native to Australia, the cool, clean waters of Tasmania make an ideal environment for farming salmon.

Salmon is naturally rich in essential vitamins and minerals and a rich source of omega-3 fatty acids, which are important for healthy hearts and minds but cannot be produced by our bodies. It is recommended that we eat at least two fish-based meals per week, but today people still don't eat enough fish. The popularity and versatility of salmon is beginning to change this.

Buying salmon

Tasmanian Atlantic salmon is readily available in many forms and cuts, to suit different recipes and preparation methods. A dressed salmon is a whole fish with gills and guts removed. Pan-dressed means that it also has its head, tail, fins and scales removed and it is ready to cook. Salmon steaks or cutlets are cross-section slices which are ready to cook but contain skin and bones. Fillets refer to individual-sized portions that are cut from the side of the salmon. Fillets are usually boneless but should always be checked for small pin bones which can be removed with tweezers. Fillets can be bought with or without skin. They are ready to cook, or can easily be cut into cubes or slices depending on the recipe.

Choosing salmon

When buying a whole salmon, make sure the eyes are clear and bright and the skin is moist.

Smell is another important indicator of freshness and quality, fresh salmon will have a pleasant ocean smell. Salmon steaks, cutlets and fillets should appear fresh-cut and moist, with no browning around the edges. The flesh of a fresh salmon should gently spring back when pressed with a finger.

Cooking salmon

Produced in one of the purest and most pristine environments in the world, Tasmanian Atlantic salmon has become our preferred eating fish. With its rich flavour and robust texture, salmon can be cooked in a variety of ways- baked, barbecued, roasted, poached, grilled, steamed or fried. The meatiness of the salmon ensures that it barbecues especially well.

Storing salmon

Fresh salmon can be kept for up to two days in the fridge (though this will depend on the freshness of the salmon when purchased).

Salmon is an ideal fish for freezing, due to its meatiness. It must be wrapped in plastic or stored in an airtight container when freezing to retain its moisture. Salmon should always be thawed in the fridge; it is not safe to thaw at room temperature or in warm water.

salmon carpaccio

Cut the salmon as thinly as you like. Freezing the piece of salmon for about 1 hour will make it easier to slice it finely. You can finely slice the partly frozen fish using a mandoline or V-slicer.

½ medium green capsicum (bell pepper) (100g), diced finely

2 green onions (scallions), chopped finely

400g (12½-ounce) piece sashimi salmon, sliced thinly

1 tablespoon fresh dill sprigs

2 tablespoons lime juice

2 tablespoons extra virgin olive oil

1 Combine capsicum and onion in small bowl.
2 Arrange salmon slices on large serving plate. Sprinkle capsicum mixture on salmon; top with dill. Drizzle salmon with juice, then oil. Season.
3 Cover salmon; refrigerate 1 hour.

prep time 20 minutes (+ refrigeration) **serves** 8
nutritional count per serving 8.1g total fat (1.4g saturated fat); 479kJ (114 cal); 0.4g carbohydrate; 9.9g protein; 0.1g fibre
serving suggestions Scatter micro leaves over salmon. Serve with thinly sliced toasted bread.

garlic & chilli mussels

60g (2 ounces) butter, chopped coarsely

3 cloves garlic, chopped finely

1 fresh long red chilli, sliced thinly

⅓ cup (80ml) dry white wine

1kg (2 pounds) cleaned small black mussels

⅓ cup coarsely chopped fresh flat-leaf parsley

1 Heat butter, garlic and chilli in large saucepan, stirring, until fragrant. Add wine; bring to the boil.
2 Add mussels to pan; simmer, covered, until mussels open. Stir in parsley; season to taste.

prep + cook time 10 minutes **serves** 4
nutritional count per serving 13.3g total fat (8.4g saturated fat); 702kJ (168 cal); 2.8g carbohydrate; 6.3g protein; 0.6g fibre
tip To save time, use pre-cleaned, bearded mussels.
serving suggestion Serve with crusty bread or a bowl of french fries.

salt-baked fish with gremolata

2.4kg (4¾-pound) cleaned whole ocean trout

3kg (6 pounds) coarse cooking salt (kosher salt)

4 egg whites

1.5kg (3 pounds) baby new potatoes

4 cloves garlic, unpeeled

1 tablespoon olive oil

10 sprigs fresh lemon thyme

350g (11 ounces) watercress, trimmed

GREMOLATA

½ cup finely chopped fresh flat-leaf parsley

1 tablespoon finely grated lemon rind

1 tablespoon lemon juice

1 clove garlic, chopped finely

1 Preheat oven to 200°C/400°F.

2 Pat fish dry, inside and out, with absorbent paper.

3 Combine salt and egg whites in medium bowl. Spread half the salt mixture evenly over base of large baking dish; place fish on salt mixture, cover fish completely (except for tail) with remaining salt mixture. Bake 1 hour.

4 Meanwhile, combine potatoes, garlic, oil and thyme in large shallow baking dish; place in oven on shelf below fish. Bake about 50 minutes or until potatoes are tender.

5 Make gremolata.

6 Remove fish from oven; break salt crust with heavy knife, taking care not to cut into fish. Discard salt crust. Transfer fish to large serving plate; carefully remove skin from fish. Sprinkle gremolata on fish.

7 Serve fish with potatoes and watercress.

gremolata Combine ingredients in small bowl.

prep + cook time 1 hour 20 minutes **serves** 6
nutritional count per serving 6.7g total fat (1.5g saturated fat); 1680kJ (402 cal); 33.4g carbohydrate; 47.8g protein; 6.9g fibre
tip Covering the fish with salt for baking ensures all the steam gets trapped inside to keep the fish beautifully moist.
serving suggestion Serve with lemon wedges.

scallop & rocket salad

12 scallops without roe (300g)

75g (2½ ounces) baby rocket (arugula) leaves

1 lebanese cucumber (130g), sliced thinly lengthways

1 tablespoon sesame seeds, toasted

1 lime, cut into wedges

BALSAMIC DRESSING

1 tablespoon balsamic vinegar

1 teaspoon olive oil

1 teaspoon lime juice

pinch white (granulated) sugar

1 Make balsamic dressing.

2 Pat scallops dry with absorbent paper. Cook scallops on heated oiled grill pan (or grill or barbecue) until browned lightly both sides. Remove from heat; cover to keep warm.

3 Place rocket, cucumber and dressing in medium bowl; toss gently to combine.

4 Divide salad among serving plates; top with scallops and sesame seeds. Serve with lime wedges.

balsamic dressing Place ingredients in screw-top jar, season to taste; shake well.

prep + cook time 15 minutes **serves** 4
nutritional count per serving 3.1g total fat (0.4g saturated fat); 222kJ (53 cal); 1.3g carbohydrate; 4.5g protein; 0.8g fibre
tips Always choose fresh scallops rather than frozen ones, as the frozen scallops are gorged with water and tend to stew rather than grill when cooked. We used a vegetable peeler to slice the cucumber thinly into ribbons.

chilli salt prawns

1kg (2 pounds) uncooked medium
king prawns (shrimp)

1 tablespoon olive oil

2 teaspoons sea salt flakes

½ teaspoon dried chilli flakes

1 teaspoon finely chopped fresh flat-leaf parsley

YOGURT DIPPING SAUCE

1 cup (280g) yogurt

2 tablespoons mayonnaise

1 tablespoon finely grated lemon rind

1 tablespoon lemon juice

1 Preheat oven to 220°C/425°F. Oil oven tray;
line with baking paper.
2 Make yogurt dipping sauce.
3 Shell and devein prawns, leaving tails intact.
4 Combine prawns, oil, salt and chilli on tray;
spread prawns into single layer. Cook prawns
about 10 minutes.
5 Sprinkle parsley over sauce; serve with prawns.
yogurt dipping sauce Combine ingredients in
small bowl.

prep + cook time 20 minutes **serves** 4
nutritional count per serving 10.9g total fat
(2.7g saturated fat); 991kJ (237 cal);
5.5g carbohydrate; 29.1g protein; 0.2g fibre
tip You can also barbecue the prawns but they will
take only a few minutes to cook.
serving suggestion Serve with a green leafy salad.

balmain bug salad

150g (4½ ounces) thick rice stick noodles

8 uncooked shelled balmain bug tails (650g)

2 cloves garlic, crushed

1 tablespoon finely chopped fresh coriander (cilantro)

2 tablespoons vegetable oil

½ medium green papaya (500g), grated coarsely

2 fresh long red chillies, chopped finely

1 tablespoon fish sauce

⅓ cup (80ml) lime juice

⅔ cup loosely packed fresh coriander (cilantro) leaves

1 Place noodles in medium heatproof bowl, cover with boiling water; stand 20 minutes. Drain.

2 Meanwhile, combine bug tails, garlic, chopped coriander and half the oil in large bowl. Cook bug tail mixture in large heated frying pan until tails are changed in colour.

3 Combine remaining ingredients with noodles in large bowl; add warm bug tails, mix gently.

prep + cook time 30 minutes **serves** 4
nutritional count per serving 10.7g total fat
(1.4g saturated fat); 1200kJ (287 cal);
15g carbohydrate; 31g protein; 2.8g fibre
tips Balmain bugs are a type of crayfish, and are also known as slipper, shovelnose or southern bay lobster. Substitute balmain bugs with king prawns, lobster, scampi or moreton bay bugs, if you prefer. We used baby coriander leaves, but the regular size is fine to use too.

stir-fried salt & pepper squid

1kg (2 pounds) squid hoods

½ cup (75g) cornflour (cornstarch)

2 teaspoons sea salt flakes

2 teaspoons finely grated lemon rind

2 teaspoons freshly ground peppercorn medley

2 tablespoons vegetable oil

1 Cut squid down centre to open out; score inside in a diagonal pattern. Halve squid lengthways; cut into 5cm (2-inch) pieces.

2 Combine squid, cornflour, salt, rind and pepper in large bowl.

3 Heat oil in large wok; stir-fry squid, in batches, until tender and golden.

prep + cook time 30 minutes **serves** 4
nutritional count per serving 12.3g total fat (2.2g saturated fat); 1430kJ (342 cal); 15.7g carbohydrate; 41.8g protein; 0.1g fibre
tip Peppercorn medley is a mix of black, white, green and pink peppercorns, coriander seeds and allspice. It is sold in disposable grinders in supermarkets.
serving suggestion Serve with lemon wedges and a rocket (arugula) salad.

perfect fish 'n' chips

vegetable oil, for deep-frying

750g (1½ pounds) potatoes, peeled, cut into fingers

750g (1½ pounds) firm white fish fillets,
cut into 8 pieces

1 cup (150g) plain (all-purpose) flour

BATTER

1½ cups (225g) self-raising flour

½ cup (75g) cornflour (cornstarch)

1½ cups (375ml) chilled beer

¼ cup (60ml) chilled soda water

1 Make batter.

2 Heat oil in large saucepan; cook chips, in two batches, 4 minutes each or until just tender but not browned. Drain on absorbent paper; stand 10 minutes.

3 Reheat oil; cook chips, in batches, until crisp and golden brown. Drain on absorbent paper.

4 Toss fish in flour; shake away any excess. Dip fish in batter; drain off excess.

5 Reheat oil; cook fish, in batches, 4 minutes each or until golden. Drain on absorbent paper.

batter Sift flours into large bowl; gradually whisk in beer and soda water to form a thin batter. Refrigerate 30 minutes.

prep + cook time 50 minutes (+ refrigeration)
serves 4
nutritional count per serving 14.3g total fat
(2.6g saturated fat); 3285kJ (785 cal);
103.8g carbohydrate; 51.8g protein; 6.4g fibre
tips Rinse cut potatoes in cold water to remove starch. Drain well; pat dry with absorbent paper. You can use any firm white fish you prefer such as whiting or flathead.
serving suggestion Serve with tartare sauce and lemon wedges.

South Coast, New South Wales

BARBECUES & GRILLS Barbecued meals are everything we love about summer food: they're fresh, simple, quick and delicious. What's more, it's a pleasure to be outside on a summer's evening, chatting while you cook.

grilled lemon chicken

½ cup (125ml) olive oil

½ cup (125ml) lemon juice

1.5kg (3 pounds) chicken thigh fillets

2 teaspoons rigani

2 teaspoons coarse cooking salt (kosher salt)

1 teaspoon ground white pepper

1 medium lemon (140g)

1 tablespoon fresh oregano leaves

1 Blend or process oil and juice until mixture is thick and creamy.

2 Combine chicken, rigani, salt, pepper and half the lemon mixture in medium bowl. Thread chicken onto eight oiled metal skewers.

3 Cook skewers on heated oiled barbecue (or grill or grill plate), brushing frequently with remaining lemon mixture until cooked through.

4 Serve skewers, sprinkled with oregano and lemon wedges.

prep + cook time 30 minutes **makes** 8
nutritional count per skewer 30g total fat
(7g saturated fat); 1690kJ (404 cal);
1g carbohydrate; 33g protein; 0.1g fibre
tip Rigani is dried Greek oregano, sold in bunches in Greek, Portuguese and Italian stores. You can use dried oregano instead.
serving suggestion Serve with a green leaf salad.

portuguese chickens with fig salad

170g (5½ ounces) bottled roasted red capsicum (bell peppers), drained

½ cup loosely packed fresh coriander (cilantro) leaves

¼ cup (90g) honey

¼ cup (60ml) olive oil

1 tablespoon balsamic vinegar

1 tablespoon finely grated lemon rind

1 tablespoon lemon juice

4 whole dried long red chillies

4 x 500g (1-pound) small chickens, butterflied

FIG SALAD

2 tablespoons white balsamic vinegar

2 tablespoons lemon-infused olive oil

60g (2 ounces) baby spinach leaves

4 large figs (320g), quartered

½ cup (40g) shaved parmesan cheese

1 Blend or process capsicum, coriander, honey, oil, vinegar, rind, juice and chilli until smooth. Combine capsicum mixture with chickens in large bowl. Cover; refrigerate 3 hours or overnight.

2 Season chickens; cook on heated oiled barbecue (or grill or grill pan) about 20 minutes or until cooked through. Remove from barbecue; cover chickens, stand 10 minutes.

3 Make fig salad.

4 Cut chickens into serving-sized pieces; serve with salad.

fig salad Place vinegar and oil in screw-top jar; shake well, season. Place remaining ingredients in large bowl with dressing; toss gently to combine.

prep + cook time 40 minutes (+ refrigeration)
serves 4
nutritional count per serving 65.9g total fat (17.6g saturated fat); 3854kJ (922 cal); 27.2g carbohydrate; 55.3g protein; 3.2g fibre
tip Butterflied small chickens are available from specialist chicken and butcher shops.

spicy yogurt chicken drumettes with raita

20 chicken drumettes (1.4kg)

½ teaspoon dried chilli flakes

1 tablespoon each ground coriander and ground cumin

2 teaspoons ground turmeric

1½ cups (420g) yogurt

½ cup each finely chopped fresh mint and fresh coriander (cilantro)

1 clove garlic, crushed

1 tablespoon lemon juice

1 Combine chicken with chilli, spices and half the yogurt in large bowl; season. Cover; refrigerate 30 minutes.
2 Remove chicken from marinade; shake off excess. Discard marinade. Cook chicken on heated oiled barbecue (or grill or grill pan) until cooked through.
3 Meanwhile, make raita by combining herbs, garlic, juice and remaining yogurt in small bowl.
4 Serve chicken with raita.

prep + cook time 35 minutes (+ refrigeration)
serves 4
nutritional count per serving 15.4g total fat (6.3g saturated fat); 1509kJ (361 cal); 7.9g carbohydrate; 46.4g protein; 0.6g fibre
tip To avoid burning the chicken before it's cooked through, heat the barbecue on medium.

cajun chicken burgers

2 chicken breast fillets (400g)

2 tablespoons cajun seasoning

4 crusty bread rolls (200g)

⅓ cup (95g) yogurt

2 teaspoons finely grated lemon rind

1 medium tomato (150g), chopped finely

1 shallot (25g), chopped finely

½ small ripe avocado (100g), chopped finely

50g (1½ ounces) mesclun

1 Cut chicken in half horizontally; sprinkle all over with seasoning. Cook on heated oiled barbecue (or grill or grill pan).
2 Meanwhile, cut rolls in half; toast, cut-sides down, on barbecue.
3 Combine yogurt and rind in small bowl.
4 Combine tomato, shallot and avocado in small bowl; season.
5 Sandwich mesclun, avocado mixture, chicken and yogurt mixture between rolls.

prep + cook time 30 minutes **makes** 4
nutritional count per burger 12.9g total fat (3.3g saturated fat); 1731kJ (414 cal); 41.8g carbohydrate; 30.2g protein; 3.7g fibre
tip For fish burgers, replace the chicken with four 125g (4-ounce) firm white fish fillets.

sticky pork ribs

2kg (4 pounds) american-style pork spare ribs

1 cup (280g) barbecue sauce

2 tablespoons worcestershire sauce

1 tablespoon dijon mustard

1 Preheat oven to 160°C/325°F. Line large shallow baking dish with baking paper.

2 Cut pork into portions of five or six ribs. Combine sauces and mustard in large bowl; reserve a quarter of the marinade. Add pork to bowl with marinade; turn to coat. Transfer pork to baking dish; cover with foil.

3 Roast pork 1 hour. Increase oven to 200°C/400°F. Baste pork with reserved marinade; roast further 30 minutes, uncovered, basting occasionally, or until pork is browned and sticky.

prep + cook time 1 hour 45 minutes **serves** 4
nutritional count per serving 17.1g total fat (6.5g saturated fat); 2337kJ (559 cal); 33.3g carbohydrate; 68.3g protein; 1g fibre
tip We used an oven for this recipe but you can use a hooded barbecue as an oven. Use the temperature gauge and indirect heat to avoid burning the pork.
serving suggestion Serve with baked potatoes and salad leaves.

chilli & citrus pork chops with orange watercress salad

¼ cup (60ml) lime juice

2 fresh small red thai (serrano) chillies, chopped finely

2 cloves garlic, crushed

½ cup (170g) orange marmalade

⅓ cup finely chopped fresh coriander (cilantro)

½ cup (125ml) tequila

8 pork loin chops (2.2kg)

ORANGE WATERCRESS SALAD

2 large oranges (600g)

¼ cup (60ml) lime juice

¼ cup (85g) orange marmalade

2 tablespoons olive oil

2 teaspoons tequila

100g (3 ounces) watercress, trimmed

1 medium avocado (250g), sliced thinly

½ cup loosely packed fresh coriander (cilantro) leaves

1 Combine juice, chilli, garlic, marmalade, coriander, tequila and pork in large bowl. Cover; refrigerate overnight.
2 Make orange watercress salad.
3 Drain pork; reserve marinade. Cook pork on heated oiled grill plate (or grill or barbecue), brushing occasionally with marinade, until cooked as desired.
4 Serve pork with salad.
orange watercress salad Segment oranges over large bowl; stir in lime juice, marmalade and oil. Add remaining ingredients; toss gently to combine. Season to taste.

prep + cook time 30 minutes (+ refrigeration)
serves 4
nutritional count per serving 25.2g total fat (5.5g saturated fat); 3461kJ (828 cal); 51.3g carbohydrate; 80.1g protein; 4.7g fibre
tip Do not over-cook the pork or it will be dry, it should be just slightly pink inside.

grilled steaks with anchovy butter & lemony potato wedges

2 tablespoons olive oil

6 x 220g (7-ounce) new-york cut steaks

LEMONY POTATO WEDGES

1.5kg (3 pounds) potatoes

¼ cup (60ml) olive oil

2 cloves garlic, crushed

1 tablespoon finely grated lemon rind

2 teaspoons sea salt flakes

ANCHOVY BUTTER

80g (2½ ounces) butter, softened

6 drained anchovy fillets, chopped coarsely

2 cloves garlic, crushed

2 tablespoons finely chopped fresh flat-leaf parsley

1 Make lemony potato wedges.

2 Meanwhile, make anchovy butter.

3 About 10 minutes before wedges are cooked, brush oil all over steaks; cook on heated barbecue (or grill or grill pan) until cooked as desired. Cover steaks; stand 5 minutes.

4 Serve steaks topped with a slice of anchovy butter and potato wedges.

lemony potato wedges Preheat oven to 220°C/425°F. Line oven tray with baking paper. Cut potatoes lengthways into eight wedges; boil, steam or microwave until slightly softened. Drain; pat dry with absorbent paper. Combine potato in large bowl with oil, garlic, rind and salt. Place wedges, in single layer, on tray; roast about 50 minutes or until browned lightly.

anchovy butter Mash ingredients in small bowl with fork until well combined. Roll mixture tightly in plastic wrap to make a log; refrigerate until firm.

prep + cook time 1 hour **serves** 6
nutritional count per serving 39.8g total fat (14.9g saturated fat); 2989kJ (715 cal); 33.1g carbohydrate; 53.7g protein; 5.5g fibre
tips New-York cut steak is sometimes called boneless sirloin by butchers. Make the anchovy butter a day, or even a month or so, ahead, if you like, and freeze it.

beef & reef with tarragon butter

90g (3 ounces) butter, softened

2 cloves garlic, crushed

1 tablespoon finely chopped fresh tarragon

2 teaspoons dijon mustard

12 uncooked medium king prawns (shrimp) (540g)

4 x 250g (8-ounce) beef rib-eye (scotch fillet) steaks, bone in

185g (6 ounces) asparagus

1 Combine butter, garlic, tarragon and mustard in small bowl. Place butter mixture on a piece of plastic wrap; shape into log, wrap tightly. Freeze about 1 hour or until firm; remove 15 minutes before serving.

2 Shell and devein prawns, leaving tails intact.

3 Cook steaks on heated oiled barbecue (or grill or grill pan). Remove steaks from barbecue; cover, stand 5 minutes.

4 Cook prawns and asparagus on heated oiled barbecue (or grill or grill pan).

5 Serve beef topped with sliced tarragon butter, prawns and asparagus.

prep + cook time 35 minutes (+ freezing) **serves** 4
nutritional count per serving 32.2g total fat
(17.8g saturated fat); 2169kJ (519 cal);
0.8g carbohydrate; 56.8g protein; 0.8g fibre

grilled lamb chops
with tomato & olive salsa

¼ cup loosely packed fresh oregano leaves

8 lamb loin chops (800g)

100g (3 ounces) rocket (arugula) leaves

TOMATO & OLIVE SALSA

250g (8 ounces) cherry tomatoes, quartered

½ cup (60g) seeded black olives, halved

2 tablespoons french dressing

1 Finely chop half the oregano; combine with lamb in large bowl. Season.

2 Cook lamb on heated oiled barbecue (or grill or grill pan) until cooked as desired.

3 Meanwhile, make tomato & olive salsa.

4 Serve lamb with salsa and rocket.

tomato & olive salsa Combine ingredients in medium bowl.

prep + cook time 10 minutes **serves** 4
nutritional count per serving 16.2g total fat (6.6g saturated fat); 1333kJ (319 cal); 8.2g carbohydrate; 33.9g protein; 2.2g fibre

lobster with lime & herbs

6 uncooked medium lobster tails (2.5kg)

⅓ cup (80ml) olive oil

2 teaspoons finely grated lime rind

½ cup (125ml) lime juice

2 cloves garlic, crushed

2 tablespoons each coarsely chopped fresh coriander (cilantro) and flat-leaf parsley

6 limes, cut into wedges

1 Remove and discard soft shell from underneath lobster tails to expose flesh.
2 Combine oil, rind, juice, garlic and herbs in large bowl; add lobster, season. Cover; refrigerate 1 hour.
3 Drain lobster; reserve marinade.
4 Cook lobster on heated oiled barbecue until browned all over and cooked through, brushing lobster occasionally with reserved marinade during cooking. Serve with lime wedges.

prep + cook time 35 minutes (+ refrigeration)
serves 6
nutritional count per serving 15g total fat (2.3g saturated fat); 1701kJ (407 cal); 1g carbohydrate; 66g protein; 1.4g fibre
tip Do not over-cook lobster or it will be dry.

Vaucluse Sailing Club, New South Wales

dukkah prawn skewers

1.2kg (2½ pounds) uncooked large
king prawns (shrimp)

¼ cup (35g) pistachio dukkah

2 tablespoons olive oil

2 cloves garlic, crushed

2 teaspoons finely grated lemon rind

1 Shell and devein prawns, leaving tails intact.
2 Combine dukkah, oil, garlic and rind in large
bowl, add prawns; toss to coat in dukkah mixture.
3 Thread prawns onto eight bamboo skewers.
Cook skewers on heated oiled grill plate (or grill or
barbecue) until prawns change colour.

prep + cook time 15 minutes **serves** 4
nutritional count per serving 14.5g total fat (2g
saturated fat); 1124kJ (269 cal); 1.5g carbohydrate;
32.6g protein; 1.1g fibre
tips You can buy prawns already shelled from
the fishmonger. Dukkah can be found in the spice
aisle of supermarkets. Soak bamboo skewers in
cold water for 1 hour to prevent splintering and
scorching during cooking.
serving suggestion Serve with lemon wedges and
a mixed leaf salad.

ICE-CREAM & GELATO Frozen treats are such a fabulous dessert option in summer. The kids adore them, they go beautifully with the fruits of the season, and best of all, you can prepare them in advance for easy entertaining.

raspberry nougat frozen parfait

2 cups (400g) ricotta cheese

¾ cup (165g) caster (superfine) sugar

¼ cup (40g) whole almonds, roasted, chopped coarsely

150g (4½ ounces) nougat, chopped coarsely

1¼ cups (310ml) thickened (heavy) cream

1 cup (135g) frozen raspberries

1 Line base and sides of 14cm x 21cm (5½-inch x 8½-inch) loaf pan with foil or baking paper, extending foil 5cm (2 inches) over two long sides.
2 Blend or process cheese and sugar until smooth; transfer to large bowl. Stir in nuts and nougat.
3 Beat cream in small bowl with electric mixer until soft peaks form. Fold cream into cheese mixture; fold in raspberries.
4 Spoon mixture into pan, cover with foil; freeze until firm.
5 Slice parfait, then refrigerate about 30 minutes before serving, to soften slightly.

prep + cook time 25 minutes (+ freezing & refrigeration) **serves** 8
nutritional count per serving 24.5g total fat (13.5g saturated fat); 1329kJ (318 cal); 37.4g carbohydrate; 8.1g protein; 1.4g fibre

tips It is fine to use just one 300ml carton of cream for this recipe. The parfait can be made a week ahead up to step 3; slice with a knife that has been dipped in hot water, before allowing to soften in the refrigerator (step 5).
serving suggestion Serve with fresh raspberries. You can serve it with a raspberry compote: cook 2½ cups (330g) frozen raspberries and ¼ cup (55g) caster (superfine) sugar in medium saucepan, stirring, over low heat, until berries are very soft. Push mixture through coarse sieve into medium bowl; discard seeds. Just before serving, stir 500g (1 pound) fresh raspberries into berry sauce.

nougat semifreddo with orange & honey syrup

1 vanilla bean

3 eggs, separated

⅓ cup (75g) caster (superfine) sugar

1½ cups (375ml) thickened (heavy) cream

200g (6½ ounces) nougat, chopped finely

½ cup (75g) coarsely chopped toasted shelled pistachios

1 tablespoon honey

ORANGE HONEY SYRUP

¼ cup (90g) honey

1 tablespoon finely grated orange rind

2 tablespoons orange juice

1 Split vanilla bean in half lengthways; scrape seeds into small bowl, reserve pod for another use. Add yolks and sugar; beat with electric mixer until thick and creamy. Transfer mixture to large bowl.

2 Beat cream in small bowl with electric mixer until soft peaks form; gently fold cream into yolk mixture.

3 Beat egg whites in separate small bowl with electric mixer until soft peaks form. Gently fold half the egg whites into cream mixture; fold in nougat, nuts, honey and remaining egg white. Spoon mixture into loaf pan or stainless steel bowl, cover with foil; freeze 3 hours or until just firm.

4 Make orange honey syrup.

5 Stand semifreddo at room temperature 10 minutes before serving with syrup.

orange honey syrup Bring ingredients to the boil in small saucepan. Reduce heat; simmer, uncovered, 2 minutes.

prep + cook time 25 minutes (+ freezing) **serves** 4
nutritional count per serving 51.6g total fat (25.5g saturated fat); 3532kJ (845 cal); 87g carbohydrate; 13.3g protein; 2.2g fibre
tips A traditional Italian dessert, semifreddo loosely translates as "a bit cold", and can refer to any partially frozen sweet served at the end of a meal. Using the actual bean imparts the real taste of aromatic vanilla to a recipe.

coconut & mango ice blocks with biscuit sand

1¼ cups (310ml) coconut cream

1 vanilla bean

½ cup (110g) caster (superfine) sugar

1 cup (250ml) water

1 small mango (300g), chopped coarsely

250g (8 ounces) plain sweet biscuits

8 ice block sticks

1 Pour coconut cream into small saucepan; split vanilla bean lengthways, scrape seeds into pan. Bring to the boil; remove from heat, strain into small jug. Cool.
2 Divide mixture between eight ½-cup (125ml) ice block moulds. Freeze about 2 hours or until solid.
3 Combine sugar and the water in small saucepan, stirring over high heat until sugar is dissolved; bring to the boil. Reduce heat; simmer 1 minute.
4 Blend or process mango and hot sugar syrup until smooth; cool.
5 Pour mango mixture into moulds. Cover moulds tightly with plastic wrap, push sticks through plastic into mango mixture until three-quarters of the way into ice block. Freeze overnight.
6 Blend or process biscuits until fine. Serve ice blocks with bowls of biscuit sand for dipping.

prep + cook time 30 minutes (+ freezing) **makes** 8
nutritional count per ice block 12.5g total fat
(9.1g saturated fat); 1180kJ (282 cal);
40.6g carbohydrate; 2.9g protein; 1.3g fibre
tip To un-mould ice blocks remove from freezer and stand 5 minutes. Wrap each ice block in a hot damp tea towel until ice block becomes loose.

raspberry, lemon & mint ice blocks

½ cup (110g) caster (superfine) sugar

1 cup (250ml) water

1¾ cups (375ml) lemonade

1 tablespoon lemon juice

125g (4 ounces) fresh raspberries

40 small fresh mint leaves

8 ice block sticks

1 Combine sugar and the water in small saucepan, stirring over high heat until sugar is dissolved; bring to the boil. Remove from heat; cool.
2 Place four raspberries and five mint leaves into each of eight ½-cup (125ml) ice block moulds. Push remaining raspberries through a fine sieve; discard seeds. Reserve puree.
3 Combine sugar syrup, lemonade and juice in medium jug; pour into moulds, leaving 1cm (½-inch) gap from the top.
4 Spoon pureed raspberries into moulds – do not stir. Cover moulds tightly with plastic wrap, push sticks through plastic into mixture until three-quarters of the way into ice block. Freeze overnight.

prep + cook time 30 minutes (+ freezing) **makes** 8
nutritional count per ice block 0.1g total fat
(0g saturated fat); 329kJ (79 cal);
19.8g carbohydrate; 0.2g protein; 0.8g fibre
tip To un-mould ice blocks remove from freezer and stand 5 minutes. Wrap each ice block in a hot damp tea towel until ice block becomes loose.

raspberry bombe alaska

1.5 litres (6 cups) vanilla ice-cream,
softened slightly

1 cup (135g) frozen raspberries

1 tablespoon caster (superfine) sugar

200g (6½ ounces) madeira cake

4 egg whites

1 cup (220g) firmly packed light brown sugar

1 teaspoon vanilla extract

1 teaspoon cornflour (cornstarch)

1 Line four ¾-cup (180ml) moulds with plastic
wrap. Press a quarter of the ice-cream firmly up
and around inside of each mould to form a cavity.
Cover with foil; freeze about 2 hours or until firm.

2 Preheat oven to 240°C/475°F.

3 Place raspberries and caster sugar in small
saucepan; stir gently over low heat about 5 minutes
or until sugar dissolves. Cool 15 minutes.

4 Cut cake into four thick slices; cut one round
from each quarter, large enough to cover top of
each mould.

5 Beat egg whites in small bowl with electric mixer
until soft peaks form. Gradually add brown sugar,
1 tablespoon at a time, beating until sugar dissolves
between additions. Fold in extract and cornflour.

6 Spoon a quarter of the raspberry sauce into one
mould; turn mould onto one cake round on oven
tray, peel away plastic wrap. Spread a quarter
of the meringue mixture over cake to enclose
bombe completely. Repeat with remaining moulds,
raspberry sauce, cake rounds and meringue
mixture. Bake bombes about 3 minutes or until
browned lightly.

prep + cook time 30 minutes (+ freezing & cooling)
serves 4
nutritional count per serving 28.4g total fat
(15.7g saturated fat); 3143kJ (752 cal);
116.3g carbohydrate; 13.1g protein; 2.3g fibre
tip Packaged madeira cakes, found in nearly
every supermarket, can be used as the base of
baked Alaska or for turning into cake crumbs for
rum balls. Similar to American pound cake or an
English Victoria sponge, this sweet, buttery cake
got its name in the early 1900s when it was eaten
after dinner with a glass of Madeira wine.

mangoes

Mangoes were first cultivated over 4000 years ago on the Indian subcontinent, before travelling through the Middle East, Africa, South America and the Philippines to Australia. Today, the sweet, tropical taste of a mango has come to embody the quintessential Australian summer.

The All-rounder

Mangoes are a truly versatile fruit; they are delicious in salads, cocktails, smoothies and desserts, or as a nutritious snack. Ripe mango flesh can be frozen, dried, cooked and pureed. Brimming with vitamins and calcium and a rich source of fibre and potassium, mangoes are a guilt-free treat. Mangoes are one of the few remaining truly seasonal fruits. The first sign of their sweet scent evokes memories of eating mangoes on Christmas morning over the kitchen sink, sticky juice dripping down your arms.

Australian mango varieties

Australian mangoes are grown in the tropical and subtropical regions of Northern Territory, Queensland, New South Wales and Western Australia. Queensland produces the largest mango crop of any state, and is predominantly made up of the famous Kensington Prides.

Kensington Pride (AKA Bowen) is undoubtedly the most well-known and well-loved mango variety and is available throughout the mango season from September to March. They are medium sized, with sweet soft flesh. Their orange skin is characterised by a red-pink blush. Kensington Prides make up 70% of the Australian mango crop.

Calypso mangoes have firm, fibreless flesh and a deep orange blush. Also available throughout the mango season, their firm flesh works well in salads.

R2E2s are large, mild-flavoured mangoes. They are popular exports due to their long shelf life. Available from November to February.

Honey Golds have juicy, deep-flavoured flesh and distinctive golden apricot coloured skin. They are available from November through to March. Their fibreless flesh, makes them an ideal choice for salads and smoothies.

Australian varieties that are available later in the season include Palmer, Kiett, Kent, Pearl and Brooks.

Buying mangoes

Smell is the most important indicator of ripeness when it comes to mangoes. A ripe mango has a fresh, tropical scent. An unripe mango will have no smell and an unpleasant chemical taste. The 'blush' of the mango, which refers to the colour of the skin as it ripens, should be a deep, rich colour, and a ripe mango will give slightly to the touch. Avoid mangoes that are soft and squishy as it means they are bruised or overripe. Completely green mangoes will not ripen, but are popular in South-East Asian salads.

Storing mangoes

Mangoes should be stored out of the refrigerator until ripe. This will ensure that the premium flavour is preserved. To ripen mangoes put them in a paper bag and keep them at room temperature out of direct sunlight. Never store mangoes in plastic bags as they will sweat. Mangoes will not ripen in the refrigerator but ripe mangoes can be stored there in order to keep them chilled and fresh. Properly stored mangoes will last about one week.

mango & macadamia tart
with lime syrup

¼ cup (35g) macadamias

1⅓ cups (200g) plain (all-purpose) flour

1 tablespoon caster (superfine) sugar

100g (3 ounces) cold butter, chopped coarsely

2 tablespoons iced water, approximately

2 medium mangoes (860g), sliced thinly

FILLING

2 teaspoons gelatine

2 tablespoons water

1¼ cups (310ml) thickened (heavy) cream

250g (8 ounces) cream cheese, softened

½ cup (110g) caster (superfine) sugar

1 tablespoon lime juice

LIME SYRUP

1 cup (220g) caster (superfine) sugar

½ cup (125ml) water

1 teaspoon finely grated lime rind

2 tablespoons lime juice

1 Process macadamias until ground to fine breadcrumbs.
2 Combine flour, ground macadamias, caster sugar and a little salt in large bowl; using finger tips, rub in butter until mixture resembles coarse breadcrumbs. Make a well in centre, add the water; mix until dough starts to come together. Knead dough on floured surface into a ball, flatten slightly. Wrap dough in plastic; refrigerate 20 minutes.
3 Roll pastry between two sheets of baking paper until large enough to line 11cm x 35cm (4-inch x 14-inch) loose-based rectangular fluted flan pan; refrigerate 10 minutes.
4 Grease flan pan. Lift pastry into pan, ease into base and sides; trim edge. Prick pastry base with fork; refrigerate 20 minutes.

5 Preheat oven to 200°C/400°F.
6 Line pastry with baking paper; fill with dried beans or rice. Bake 15 minutes; remove paper and beans. Bake further 20 minutes or until pastry is browned lightly. Cool.
7 Meanwhile, make filling.
8 Spread filling into tart shell. Refrigerate 4 hours or until set.
9 Make lime syrup.
10 Position overlapping mango slices on tart; drizzle with syrup.

filling Sprinkle gelatine over the water in small heatproof jug; stand jug in small saucepan of simmering water. Stir until gelatine dissolves. Cool 5 minutes. Beat cream in small bowl with electric mixer until soft peaks form. Beat cheese, sugar and juice in another small bowl with electric mixer until smooth. Stir in gelatine mixture; fold in cream.

lime syrup Stir sugar and the water in small saucepan, over high heat, without boiling, until sugar is dissolved. Bring to the boil. Reduce heat; simmer 5 minutes. Remove from heat; stir in rind and juice.

prep + cook time 1 hour 30 minutes (+ refrigeration & cooling) **serves** 10
nutritional count per serving 31g total fat (18.7g saturated fat); 2183kJ (521 cal); 56.3g carbohydrate; 6.5g protein; 1.9g fibre
tips It is fine to use just one 300ml carton of cream for this recipe. You can make the pastry using a food processor. Process flour, ground macadamias, sugar, salt and butter until coarse breadcrumbs; with motor running, add water. Process until dough comes together. As the pastry is very short, it's important to refrigerate it between steps so it's easier to handle.

coconut berry ice blocks

300g (9½ ounces) frozen raspberries

½ cup (110g) caster (superfine) sugar

2 cups (500ml) thickened (heavy) cream

2 cups (500ml) coconut cream

16 ice block sticks

1 Stir raspberries and sugar in medium saucepan over heat until sugar dissolves; bring to the boil. Reduce heat; simmer, uncovered, about 5 minutes or until mixture thickens slightly. Transfer to small bowl; refrigerate until cold.

2 Meanwhile, beat thickened cream in small bowl with electric mixer until firm peaks form; add coconut cream, beat only until combined. Transfer mixture to large bowl.

3 Fold raspberry mixture through cream mixture until rippled through. Spoon mixture into ⅓-cup (80ml) ice block moulds; insert stick. Freeze about 4 hours or until set.

4 Remove blocks from freezer; stand about 5 minutes before removing from moulds.

prep + cook time 15 minutes (+ freezing)
makes 16
nutritional count per ice block 17.7g total fat (13.1g saturated fat); 846kJ (202 cal); 10.1g carbohydrate; 1.4g protein; 1.3g fibre
tip To un-mould ice blocks remove from freezer and stand 5 minutes. Wrap each ice block in a hot damp tea towel until ice block becomes loose.
serving suggestion Serve with fresh raspberries over ice, or with a small bowl of dessicated coconut for dipping.

ice-cream sundaes

100g (3 ounces) white mini marshmallows

2 litres (8 cups) vanilla ice-cream

½ cup (70g) crushed nuts

12 chocolate-filled wafer sticks

HOT CHOCOLATE SAUCE

200g (6½ ounces) dark eating (semi-sweet) chocolate, chopped coarsely

½ cup (125ml) thickened (heavy) cream

1 Make hot chocolate sauce.
2 Place a little of the hot chocolate sauce in the bottom of six 1½-cup (375ml) serving glasses; stick cut-sides of marshmallows to inside edge of glasses.
3 Divide ice-cream, remaining chocolate sauce, nuts and wafer sticks between glasses.
hot chocolate sauce Stir chocolate and cream in small saucepan over low heat until smooth.

prep + cook time 10 minutes **serves** 6
nutritional count per serving 50.5g total fat (30.1g saturated fat); 3520kJ (842 cal); 89.8g carbohydrate; 13.6g protein; 1.6g fibre

passionfruit & banana crush

1¼ cups (310ml) thickened (heavy) cream

2 tablespoons lemon-flavoured spread

50g (1½ ounces) mini pavlova shells, chopped coarsely

4 small bananas (520g), chopped coarsely

½ cup (125ml) passionfruit pulp

1 Beat cream and spread in small bowl with electric mixer until soft peaks form.
2 Layer lemon cream, pavlova pieces, banana and passionfruit into four serving glasses.

prep time 15 minutes **serves** 4
nutritional count per serving 28.6g total fat (18.5g saturated fat); 1839kJ (440 cal); 38.9g carbohydrate; 4.4g protein; 6.3g fibre
tips It is fine to use just one 300ml carton of cream for this recipe. Mini pavlova shells are available from most supermarkets. You need six passionfruit for this recipe.

{photograph page 340}

passionfruit & banana crush
{recipe page 339}

East coast, Victoria

GLOSSARY

ALLSPICE also called pimento or jamaican pepper; available whole or ground. Tastes like a combination of nutmeg, cumin, clove and cinnamon.

ALMONDS

flaked paper-thin slices.

ground also called almond meal.

slivered small pieces cut lengthways.

ARTICHOKE HEARTS tender centre of the globe artichoke; can be harvested from the plant after the prickly choke is removed. Cooked hearts are available from delicatessens or canned in brine.

BACON SLICES also known as bacon rashers.

BAKING PAPER also known as parchment paper or baking parchment – is a silicone-coated paper that is primarily used for lining baking pans and oven trays so cakes and biscuits won't stick, making removal easy.

BAKING POWDER a raising agent consisting mainly of two parts cream of tartar to one part bicarbonate of (baking) soda.

BEANS

borlotti also called roman beans or pink beans. Interchangeable with pinto beans due to their similar appearance – pale pink or beige with dark red streaks.

snake long (about 40cm), thin, round, fresh green beans, Asian in origin, with a taste similar to green or french beans. Used most frequently in stir-fries.

white a generic term we use for canned or dried cannellini, haricot, navy or great northern beans – those belonging to the *phaseolus vulgaris* family.

BEEF

eye-fillet tenderloin, fillet; fine texture, most expensive and extremely tender.

gravy boneless stewing beef from shin; slow-cooked, imbues stocks, soups and casseroles with a gelatine richness.

scotch fillet cut from the muscle running behind the shoulder along the spine. Also known as cube roll, cuts include standing rib roast and rib-eye.

skirt steak lean, flavourful coarse-grained cut from the inner thigh. Needs slow-cooking; good for stews or casseroles.

BICARBONATE OF SODA also called baking soda.

BREADCRUMBS, PANKO (JAPANESE) they have a lighter texture than western-style ones. Gives a crunchy texture with a delicate, pale golden colour. Can be found in Asian grocery stores and most major supermarkets.

BROCCOLINI a cross between broccoli and chinese kale; long asparagus-like stems with a long loose floret, both edible.

BUTTER we use salted butter unless stated otherwise; 125g (4 ounces) is equal to 1 stick.

CAPERBERRIES olive-sized fruit formed after the buds of the caper bush have flowered; they are usually sold pickled in a vinegar brine with stalks intact.

CAPSICUM (BELL PEPPER) also known as pepper. Discard seeds and membranes before use.

CARDAMOM a native Indian spice; purchased in pod, seed or ground form. Has a distinctive aromatic, sweetly rich flavour.

CELERIAC (CELERY ROOT) tuberous root with knobbly brown skin, white flesh and a celery-like flavour. Keep peeled celeriac in acidulated water to stop it discolouring.

CHEESE

bocconcini walnut-sized, baby mozzarella, a delicate, semi-soft cheese. Sold fresh, it spoils rapidly so will only keep, refrigerated in brine, for 1 or 2 days at the most.

kefalotyri a hard, salty cheese made from sheep and/or goat's milk. Its colour varies from white to yellow depending on the mixture of milk used in the process and its age. Great for grating over pasta or salads. Can be replaced with parmesan.

manchego a semi-firm Spanish sheep's cheese; mild when young, but after ageing for 3 months or longer, becomes a rich golden colour and develops a full, tangy flavour with the characteristic aftertaste of sheep's milk.

mascarpone Italian fresh cultured-cream product made similarly to yogurt. Whiteish to creamy yellow in colour, with a buttery-rich, luscious texture, it is soft, creamy and spreadable.

roqeufort a blue cheese with a singularly pungent taste; made only from the milk of specially bred sheep and ripened in the damp limestone caves found under the village of Roquefort-sur-Soulzon in France. Has a sticky, bone-coloured rind and, when ripe, the sharp, almost metallic-tasting interior is creamy and almost shiny.

CHICKEN

barbecued we use cooked whole barbecued chickens weighing about 900g (1¾ pounds) in our recipes. Skin discarded and bones removed, this size chicken provides 4 cups (400g) shredded meat or about 3 cups (400g) coarsely chopped meat.

drumette small fleshy part of the wing between shoulder and elbow, trimmed to resemble a drumstick.

small chicken also called poussin or spatchcock; no more than 6 weeks old, weighing a maximum of 500g (1 pound).

CHICKPEAS (GARBANZO BEANS) also called hummus or channa; an irregularly round, sandy-coloured legume. Firm texture even after cooking, a floury mouth-feel and robust nutty flavour; available canned or dried (reconstitute for several hours in cold water before use).

CHILLI use rubber gloves when preparing fresh chillies as they can burn your skin. We use unseeded chillies as the seeds contain the heat; use fewer chillies rather than seeding the lot.

CHINESE COOKING WINE also called shao hsing or chinese rice wine. Inexpensive and found in Asian food shops; if you can't find it, use mirin or sherry.

CHOCOLATE, DARK EATING (SEMI-SWEET) made of a high percentage of cocoa liquor, cocoa butter and a little added sugar.

CHORIZO SAUSAGE Spanish in origin; made of coarsely ground pork and highly seasoned with garlic and chilli.

CLOVES dried flower buds of a tropical tree; can be used whole or in ground form. They have a strong scent and taste so should be used sparingly.

COCONUT, MILK the diluted liquid from the second pressing of the white flesh of a mature coconut. Available in cans and cartons at most supermarkets.

CORIANDER (CILANTRO) also known as pak chee or chinese parsley; bright-green-leafed herb with pungent aroma and taste.

seeds are dried and sold either whole or ground, and neither form tastes remotely like the fresh leaf.

CORNFLOUR (CORNSTARCH) made from corn or wheat.

CORNICHON French for gherkin, a very small variety of cucumber.

CREAM

pouring also called pure cream. It has no additives and contains a minimum fat content of 35%.

thick (double) a dolloping cream with a minimum fat content of 45%.

thickened (heavy) a whipping cream that contains a thickener; minimum fat content of 35%.

DUCK we use whole ducks in some recipes; they are available from specialty chicken shops, markets and some supermarkets.

DUKKAH an Egyptian spice mixture made up of roasted nuts, seeds and aromatic spices.

EGGPLANT also called aubergine. Can also be purchased char-grilled, packed in oil, in jars.

EGGS if a recipe calls for raw or barely cooked eggs, exercise caution if there is a salmonella problem in your area, particularly in food eaten by children and pregnant women.

FENNEL also called finocchio or anise; a crunchy green vegetable slightly resembling celery that's eaten raw or cooked.

FIVE-SPICE POWDER fragrant mixture, usually containing ground cinnamon, cloves, star anise, sichuan pepper and fennel seeds. Available from Asian food shops and most supermarkets.

FLOUR

plain (all-purpose) unbleached wheat flour, the best for baking.

self-raising all-purpose plain or wholemeal flour with baking powder and salt added.

GAI LAN also called chinese broccoli and chinese kale; green vegetable appreciated more for its stems than its coarse leaves.

GELATINE a thickening agent. We use dried (powdered) gelatine.

GOLDEN SYRUP a by-product of refined sugar cane. Golden syrup and treacle (a thicker, darker syrup not unlike molasses) are similar sugar products.

HORSERADISH

cream commercially made paste consisting of grated horseradish, vinegar, oil and sugar.

prepared grated horseradish that has been preserved.

KAFFIR LIME LEAVES dried leaves are less potent than fresh, so double the number called for in a recipe if you substitute them for fresh leaves. A strip of fresh lime peel may be substituted for each kaffir lime leaf.

KECAP MANIS a dark, thick sweet soy sauce used in most South-East Asian cuisines.

LAMB

shank forequarter leg.

shoulder large, tasty piece having much connective tissue so is best pot-roasted or braised. Makes the best mince.

LEMON GRASS tall, clumping, lemon-smelling and tasting, sharp-edged aromatic tropical grass; the white lower part of the stem is used, finely chopped. Can be found, fresh, dried, frozen and powdered in supermarkets, Asian food shops and greengrocers.

MAPLE SYRUP distilled from the sap of sugar maple trees found only in Canada and some states in the USA. Maple-flavoured syrup is not a suitable substitute for the real thing.

MIRIN a Japanese champagne-coloured cooking wine, made of glutinous rice and alcohol. It is used just for cooking and should not be confused with sake.

MIXED SPICE a classic spice mixture generally containing caraway, allspice, coriander, cumin, nutmeg and ginger.

MIZUNA a mustard green from Japan; often found in a mesclun, but its mild, aromatic jagged green leaves can also stand alone. Refrigerate in a plastic bag, unwashed, up to five days.

MUSHROOMS

portobello are mature, fully opened swiss browns; they are larger and bigger in flavour.

shiitake, fresh also called chinese black, forest or golden oak mushrooms. A large and meaty cultivated mushroom, they have the earthiness and taste of wild mushrooms.

swiss brown also called roman or cremini. Light to dark brown with a full-bodied flavour; suited for use in casseroles or being stuffed and baked.

MUSTARD, JAPANESE hot mustard available as ready-to-use paste in tubes or powder from Asian grocery stores.

NUTMEG a strong and pungent spice. Usually purchased ground, the flavour is more intense freshly grated from the whole nut (available from spice shops).

OIL, OLIVE extra virgin and virgin are the first and second press, respectively, of ripened olives and are considered the best; the "extra light" or "light" name on other types refers to taste not fat levels.

ONIONS

green (scallions) also called, incorrectly, shallot; an immature onion picked before the bulb has formed, having a long, bright-green edible stalk.

shallots also called french shallots, golden shallots or eschalots. Small and elongated, with a brown skin, they grow in tight clusters similar to garlic.

spring crisp, narrow green-leafed tops and a round sweet white bulb larger than green onions.

OYSTER SAUCE thick, richly flavoured brown sauce made from oysters and their brine, cooked with salt and soy sauce, and thickened with starches.

PINE NUTS not a nut but a small, cream-coloured kernel from pine cones. Best roasted before use to bring out the flavour.

POMEGRANATE dark-red, leathery-skinned fresh fruit about the size of an orange filled with hundreds of seeds, each wrapped in an edible lucent-crimson pulp having a unique tangy sweet-sour flavour.

PORK, BELLY fatty cut sold in rashers or in a piece, with or without rind or bone.

RICE, SUSHI (KOSHIHIKARI) small, round-grain white rice. Substitute white short-grain rice, cook by absorption method.

SASHIMI fish sold as sashimi has to meet stringent guidelines regarding handling. Seek advice from local authorities before eating any raw seafood.

SEAFOOD

balmain bugs also called slipper or shovelnose lobster, or southern bay lobster; crustacean, a type of crayfish.

mussels buy from a reliable fish market: must be tightly closed when bought, indicating they are alive. Before cooking, scrub shells with a strong brush to remove the beards.

octopus usually tenderised before you buy them; both octopus and squid require either long slow cooking (if large) or quick cooking over high heat (if small) – anything in between will make the octopus tough and rubbery.

white fish non-oily fish; includes bream, flathead, redfish, whiting, snapper, dhufish and ling.

SILVER BEET (SWISS CHARD) also called, incorrectly, spinach; has fleshy stalks and large leaves, both of which can be prepared as for spinach.

SOY SAUCE also called sieu; made from fermented soybeans. Several variations are available in supermarkets and Asian food stores; we use japanese soy sauce unless stated otherwise.

SPINACH also called english spinach and, incorrectly, silver beet. Leaves should be added last, and cooked until barely wilted.

SPONGE FINGER BISCUITS also called savoiardi, savoy biscuits or lady's fingers; Italian-style crisp fingers made from sponge cake mixture.

STAR ANISE a dried star-shaped pod, its seeds have an astringent aniseed flavour; commonly used to flavour stocks and marinades.

SUGAR

dark brown a moist, dark brown sugar with a rich, distinctive full flavour from molasses.

demerara small-grained golden-coloured crystal sugar.

icing (confectioners') also called powdered sugar; pulverised granulated sugar crushed with a small amount of cornflour.

light brown a very soft, finely granulated sugar that retains molasses for colour and flavour.

palm also called nam tan pip or jaggery; made from the sap of the sugar palm tree. Light brown to black in colour and usually sold in rock-hard cakes; use brown sugar if unavailable.

pure icing (confectioners') also called powdered sugar.

TAMARIND the tamarind tree produces clusters of hairy brown pods, each is filled with seeds and a viscous pulp that are dried and pressed into the blocks of tamarind found in Asian food shops. Gives a sweet-sour, slightly astringent taste to marinades, pastes and sauces.

TAMARIND CONCENTRATE (or paste) commercial result of the distillation of tamarind juice into a condensed, compacted paste.

TOMATOES

bottled pasta sauce a prepared sauce; a blend of tomatoes, herbs and spices.

canned whole peeled tomatoes in natural juices; available crushed, chopped or diced. Use undrained.

paste triple-concentrated tomato puree used to flavour soups, stews and sauces.

puree canned pureed tomatoes (not tomato paste).

VANILLA

bean dried, long, thin pod from a tropical golden orchid; the minuscule black seeds inside the bean are used to impart a luscious vanilla flavour.

extract obtained from vanilla beans infused in water; a non-alcoholic version of essence.

VINEGAR

balsamic originally from Modena, Italy, there are now many on the market ranging in pungency and quality depending on how, and for how long, they have been aged. Quality can be determined up to a point by price; use the most expensive sparingly.

cider from fermented apples.

rice a colourless vinegar made from fermented rice and flavoured with sugar and salt. Also called seasoned rice vinegar; sherry can be substituted.

white made from distilled grain alcohol.

WATERCRESS one of the cress family, a large group of peppery greens used raw in salads, dips and sandwiches, or cooked in soups. Highly perishable, it must be used soon after purchase.

WITLOF (BELGIAN ENDIVE) related to and confused with chicory. A versatile vegetable, it tastes good cooked and raw.

WOMBOK (NAPA CABBAGE) also called chinese cabbage or peking; elongated in shape with pale green, crinkly leaves, is the most common cabbage in South-East Asia.

WORCESTERSHIRE SAUCE thin, dark-brown spicy sauce; used as a seasoning for meat, gravies and cocktails.

WRAPPERS wonton wrappers and gow gee or spring roll pastry sheets, made of flour, egg and water, are found in the refrigerated or freezer section of Asian food shops and many supermarkets. These come in different thicknesses and shapes.

YOGURT we use plain full-cream yogurt unless stated otherwise.

Greek-style plain yogurt strained in a cloth (muslin) to remove the whey and to give it a creamy consistency.

ZUCCHINI also called courgette; belongs to the squash family. When young, its edible flowers can be stuffed and deep-fried.

CONVERSION CHART

MEASURES

One Australian metric measuring cup holds approximately 250ml; one Australian metric tablespoon holds 20ml; one Australian metric teaspoon holds 5ml. The difference between one country's measuring cups and another's is within a two- or three-teaspoon variance, and will not affect your cooking results. North America, New Zealand and the United Kingdom use 15ml tablespoons.

All cup and spoon measurements are level.

The most accurate way of measuring dry ingredients is to weigh them. When measuring liquids, use a clear glass or plastic jug with the metric markings.

We use large eggs with an average weight of 60g.

DRY MEASURES

METRIC	IMPERIAL
15g	½oz
30g	1oz
60g	2oz
90g	3oz
125g	4oz (¼lb)
155g	5oz
185g	6oz
220g	7oz
250g	8oz (½lb)
280g	9oz
315g	10oz
345g	11oz
375g	12oz (¾lb)
410g	13oz
440g	14oz
470g	15oz
500g	16oz (1lb)
750g	24oz (1½lb)
1kg	32oz (2lb)

LIQUID MEASURES

METRIC	IMPERIAL
30ml	1 fluid oz
60ml	2 fluid oz
100ml	3 fluid oz
125ml	4 fluid oz
150ml	5 fluid oz
190ml	6 fluid oz
250ml	8 fluid oz
300ml	10 fluid oz
500ml	16 fluid oz
600ml	20 fluid oz
1000ml	1¾ pints

LENGTH MEASURES

METRIC	IMPERIAL
3mm	⅛in
6mm	¼in
1cm	½in
2cm	¾in
2.5cm	1in
5cm	2in
6cm	2½in
8cm	3in
10cm	4in
13cm	5in
15cm	6in
18cm	7in
20cm	8in
23cm	9in
25cm	10in
28cm	11in
30cm	12in (1ft)

OVEN TEMPERATURES

The oven temperatures in this book are for conventional ovens; if you have a fan-forced oven, decrease the temperature by 10-20 degrees.

	°C (CELSIUS)	°F (FAHRENHEIT)
Very slow	120	250
Slow	150	300
Moderately slow	160	325
Moderate	180	350
Moderately hot	200	400
Hot	220	425
Very hot	240	475

INDEX